DECORATING WOOD

arts and crafts collection

DECORATING
WOOD

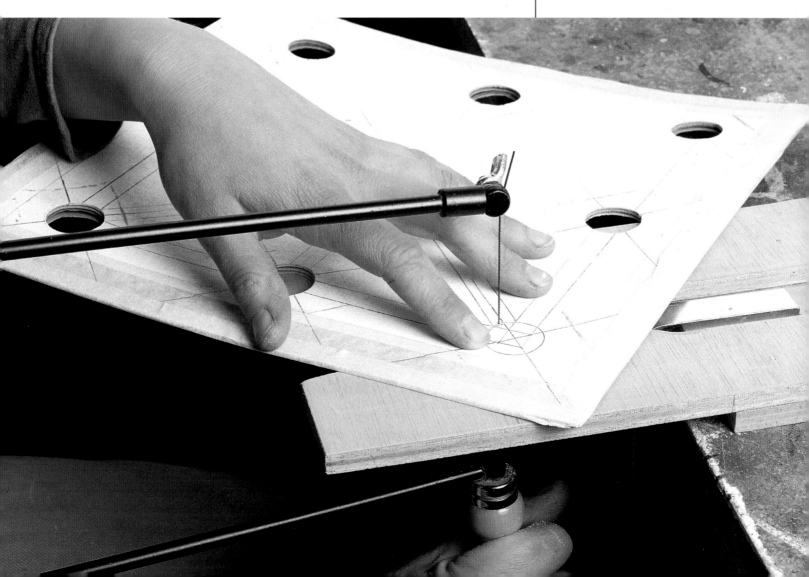

© Copyright for the English edition for
the United States, Canada, its territories
and possessions by Barron's
Educational Series, Inc. 2002

Original title of the book in Spanish:
Decoración de la Madera
© Copyright 2000 by Parramón
Ediciones, S.A.,—World Rights
Published in 2000 by Parramón
Ediciones, S.A., Barcelona, Spain

Editor: María Fernanda Canal

Text: Eva Pascual

Projects and step-by-step exercises:
Mireia Campañà: inlay and marquetry
Anna Jover: staining and bleaching
Josep Maria Miret: pyrography, veneer,
and decoupage
Eva Pascual: punching
Ana Ruiz de Conejo: painting and
gilding

Graphic design: Josep Guasch

Photography: Nos & Soto
(Josep Pascual also contributed to the
"Decorating Wood" chapter)

Illustrations: Antoni Vidal

Illustration archives: Carmen Ramos

*Translated from the Spanish by Michael
Brunelle and Beatriz Cortabarria*

All inquiries should be addressed to:
Barron's Educational Series, Inc.
250 Wireless Blvd.
Hauppauge, NY 11788
www.barronseduc.com
International Standard Book No. 0-7641-5425-7
Library of Congress Catalog Card No. 2001095380
Printed in Spain
9 8 7 6 5 4 3 2 1

Con

MATERIALS AND TOOLS, 14

TECHNICAL ASPECTS, 46

STEP BY STEP, 122

GLOSSARY, 154

BIBLIOGRAPHY AND ACKNOWLEDGMENTS, 160

Introduction

The information presented in this book is intended to serve as a manual for decorating wood. It serves as a practical guide for those who wish to learn about any technique covered in the book as well as a source of information for professionals and experts. Readers will be able to choose the chapter or subject that interests them, according to their particular needs and previous knowledge. The book explores the main techniques used for decorating wood through the history of humankind, and it explains the history and evolution for each one.

The book is divided into four chapters: decorating furniture, materials and tools, technical aspects, and step by step.

The first chapter is devoted to the techniques used for decorating furniture. A general view of the evolution of furniture is presented paralleling the decorative processes. The chapter includes a chronological chart of the main furniture styles adopted in Europe and North America from Gothic to Art Deco.

The second chapter includes a complete list of materials and tools that can be used for each decorative process. They are divided according to the decorative technique for which they are used: painting, gilding, pyrography and punching, inlay and marquetry, veneering, decoupage, and staining and bleaching. In each section corresponding to these techniques, the main characteristics are explained, as well as the way in which the materials are used, including whether they are primary or auxiliary materials. Following this, the implements and tools most commonly used for each decorative technique are discussed, as well as the auxiliary ones that have a specific and special use. Finally, the finishing materials for the decorated surface are introduced.

The third chapter covers practical examples and explains the technical aspects of decoration with illustrations of the specific processes for each technique and examples for each application—from preparing the wood to doing the final finish. The traditional processes are shown, as are the modern processes that involve new industrial materials. The history and evolution of the decorative solution is explained in the introduction for each example. The last section, which deals with safety, includes protective measures that should be observed when using dangerous products and tools.

The fourth and last chapter includes the step-by-step exercises—practical examples for decorating various types of objects. The three examples cover most of the techniques in the book and combine at least two different processes. Decorating the objects has increased their value, changed their use, or turned them into art pieces.

Finally, the glossary is a useful reference that includes the specific vocabulary covered in the book, and the bibliography a source of references for the reader who wishes to explore the subject in depth.

This book is not intended to be a complete manual for decorating wood, because the subject warrants volumes! Instead, the book provides a basic but thorough look at a series of techniques that are very different from each other but that share a common base—wood. The techniques compiled in this book do not represent all the techniques used nowadays for decorating wood, but they are the ones used throughout the history of art for decorating objects and architectural elements. This is why they are the most important and basic ones to know for people interested in this field.

We hope that this book, which is the effort of a group of professionals, serves as an introduction for those who wish to learn about furniture decorating and as a reference for those who already have some experience.

This book has been developed by a team of professionals from various disciplines, all of which are related to the field of decoration and restoration of wood.

Eva Pascual i Miró has a degree in Art History from the University of Barcelona. She specialized in Museum Studies, Design, and Conditioning at the Polytechnic University of Catalonia and in Preventive Conservation at the Autonomous University of Barcelona. She has taken courses in Market Research and Arts Management. Following her family tradition she became knowledgeable in the field of antiques, especially of furniture from Catalonia and in medieval furniture in general. She has worked for various museums and cultural institutions in Catalonia, Spain, as an archive expert, a manager of the art resources, and a coordinator of exhibits, as well as for companies offering services to cultural institutions. She is co-author of the book *Restoring Wood*, also in this collection.

Mireia Campañà i Bigorra received her education in Art History from the University of Barcelona and is a woodworker. She studied cabinetmaking for 5 years in Germany and has taken many courses in furniture restoration. She works as a cabinetmaker in a shop restoring furniture for the antique market. She also makes furniture for many stores in Barcelona, Spain.

Anna Jover i Armengol graduated from the University of Barcelona with a degree in Chemistry. She specialized in underwater archaeological restoration, particularly in wet wood, at the National Museum of Denmark in Copenhagen, and she has written numerous articles for national and international publications on the subject. She is a frequent collaborator of the Underwater Archeological Center of Catalonia. She presently owns and operates her own furniture restoration shop in Catalonia. She is co-author of the book *Furniture Restoration*, also in this collection.

Josep Maria Miret i Farré works in restoration, specializing in period furniture. Drawing on his vast knowledge, he has frequently taught furniture restoration courses to art professionals. He has frequently worked as a carpentry expert in Brittany (France) and in Huesca (Spain) restoring altarpieces. He owns and operates his own furniture restoration studio. He is co-author of the book *Furniture Restoration*, also in this collection.

Ana Ruiz de Conejo Viloria has a degree in Fine Arts from the University of Barcelona and has completed graduate work in museum studies at the École de Louvre in Paris. She has also taken courses on decorative techniques and procedures, including overglazing and transparencies. She has worked on many projects for the Béns Mobles Restoration Center of the Government of Catalonia, in the restoration of painted altarpieces in Brittany (France) and mural paintings in Trinidad (Cuba), and for companies devoted to decoration. She has also coordinated restoration work and furniture decoration.

Decorating Furniture

Furniture decoration began and developed with the history of humankind, because furniture as an artifact is an expression of humans at a particular period in history.

The first decorative motifs on furniture were without a doubt geometric. Lines and circles were carved on the surface of the wood to make designs. Even today these designs are used on rustic pieces.

Some designs have become ethnic or family symbols, and those belonging to the dominant class have become the most ornamental and symbolic decorative designs. Although furniture has always been appreciated, it is because of the decoration that many pieces become social status symbols.

Comparative Chart of Periods and Styles

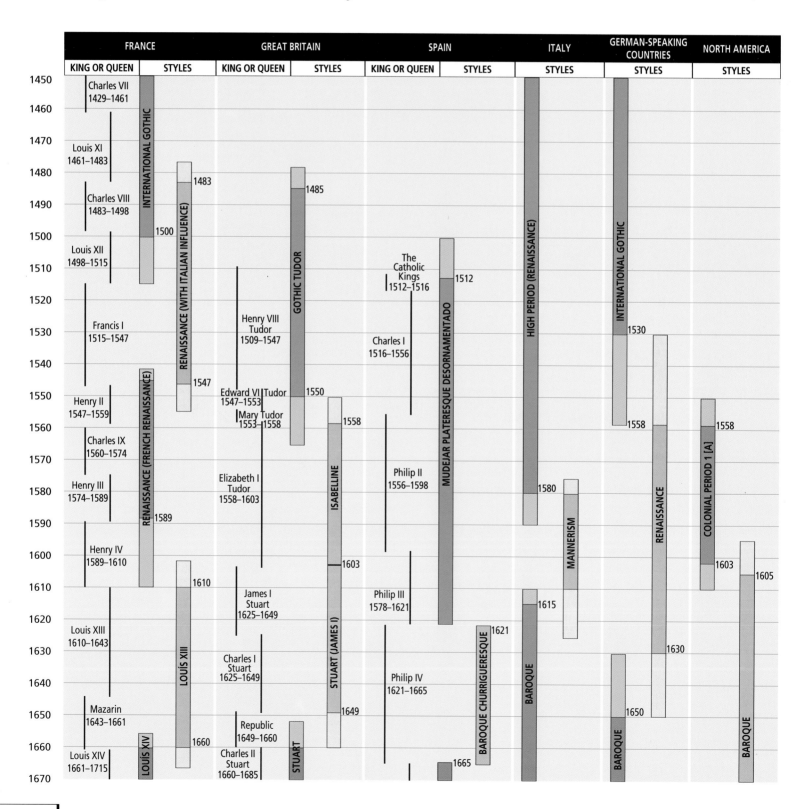

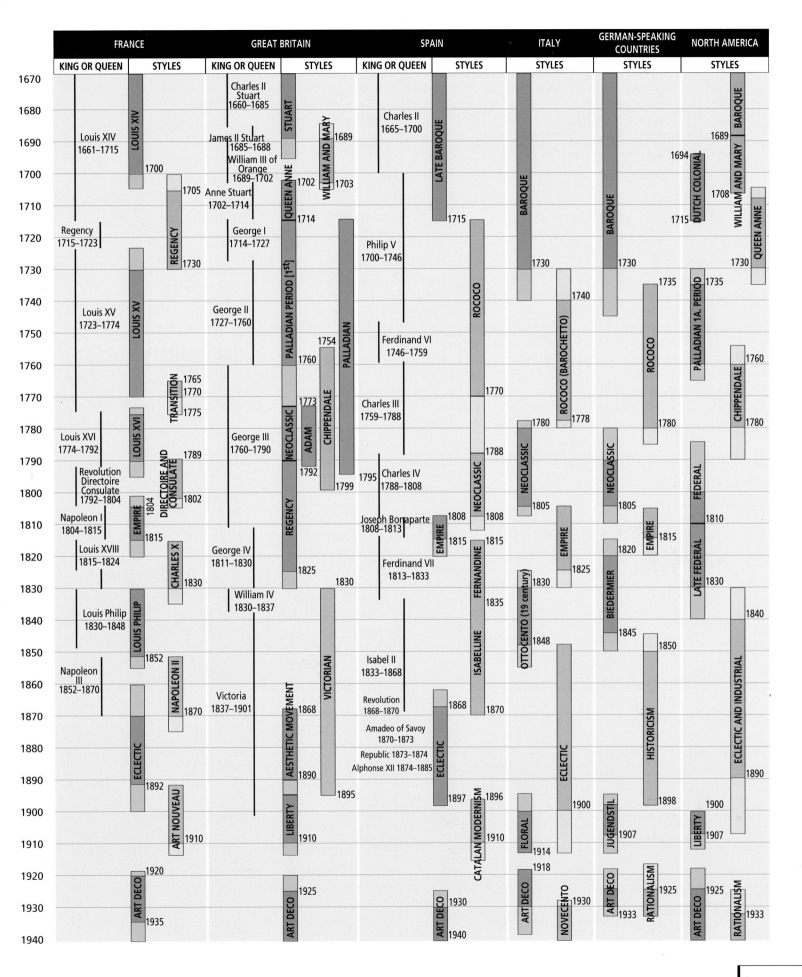

	FRANCE		GREAT BRITAIN		SPAIN		ITALY	GERMAN-SPEAKING COUNTRIES	NORTH AMERICA
	KING OR QUEEN	STYLES	KING OR QUEEN	STYLES	KING OR QUEEN	STYLES	STYLES	STYLES	STYLES

Timeline chart with years from 1670 to 1940 down the left margin.

FRANCE
- Louis XIV 1661–1715 — LOUIS XIV — 1700
- Regency 1715–1723 — REGENCY — 1705, 1730
- Louis XV 1723–1774 — LOUIS XV — TRANSITION 1765, 1770, 1775
- Louis XVI 1774–1792 — LOUIS XVI
- Revolution Directoire Consulate 1792–1804 — DIRECTOIRE AND CONSULATE — 1789, 1802
- Napoleon I 1804–1815 — EMPIRE — 1804, 1815
- Louis XVIII 1815–1824 — CHARLES X — 1830
- Louis Philip 1830–1848 — LOUIS PHILIP — 1852
- Napoleon III 1852–1870 — NAPOLEON II — 1870
- ECLECTIC — 1892
- ART NOUVEAU — 1910
- ART DECO — 1920, 1935

GREAT BRITAIN
- Charles II Stuart 1660–1685 — STUART
- James II Stuart 1685–1688 — WILLIAM AND MARY — 1689, 1702, 1703
- William III of Orange 1689–1702 — QUEEN ANNE — 1714
- Anne Stuart 1702–1714
- George I 1714–1727 — PALLADIAN PERIOD [1st] — 1754, 1760
- George II 1727–1760 — NEOCLASSIC — ADAM 1773, 1792 — CHIPPENDALE 1799
- George III 1760–1790 — REGENCY — 1825
- George IV 1811–1830 — 1830
- William IV 1830–1837 — VICTORIAN — AESTHETIC MOVEMENT 1868, 1890
- Victoria 1837–1901 — 1895 — LIBERTY 1910
- ART DECO

SPAIN
- Charles II 1665–1700 — LATE BAROQUE — 1715
- Philip V 1700–1746 — ROCOCO — 1770
- Ferdinand VI 1746–1759 — PALLADIAN
- Charles III 1759–1788 — NEOCLASSIC — 1788, 1808
- Charles IV 1788–1808 — 1795 — EMPIRE 1808, 1815
- Joseph Bonaparte 1808–1813 — FERNANDINE 1815, 1835
- Ferdinand VII 1813–1833 — ISABELLINE
- Isabel II 1833–1868 — 1868, 1870
- Revolution 1868–1870 — ECLECTIC — 1897
- Amadeo of Savoy 1870–1873
- Republic 1873–1874
- Alphonse XII 1874–1885 — CATALAN MODERNISM — 1896, 1910
- ART DECO — 1930, 1940

ITALY
- BAROQUE — 1730
- ROCOCO (BAROCHETTO) — 1740, 1780
- NEOCLASSIC — 1805
- EMPIRE — 1825
- OTTOCENTO (19 century) — 1830, 1848
- ECLECTIC — 1900
- FLORAL — 1914, 1918
- ART DECO
- NOVECENTO — 1930

GERMAN-SPEAKING COUNTRIES
- BAROQUE — 1730
- ROCOCO — 1735, 1778, 1780
- NEOCLASSIC — 1805, 1820
- EMPIRE — 1825
- BIEDERMIER — 1845, 1850
- HISTORICISM — 1898
- JUGENDSTIL — 1907
- ART DECO — 1933
- RATIONALISM — 1925

NORTH AMERICA
- BAROQUE — 1689, 1694
- DUTCH COLONIAL — 1708, 1715
- WILLIAM AND MARY — 1730
- QUEEN ANNE — 1730
- PALLADIAN 1A. PERIOD — 1735
- CHIPPENDALE — 1760, 1780
- FEDERAL — 1810
- LATE FEDERAL — 1830, 1840
- ECLECTIC AND INDUSTRIAL — 1890, 1900
- LIBERTY — 1907, 1925
- ART DECO
- RATIONALISM — 1933

Ancient Civilizations

Any information that exists about decorating furniture in acient civilization comes from illustrations and the few examples that have survived until now. In **Ancient Egypt**, decoration evolved with the construction of furniture that had elaborate structure and sophisticated style. Furniture that has survived from that period belonged either to the ruling class or to royalty and therefore is richly decorated. Techniques like gold leaf, inlay with various materials (including precious stones), and painting were the most common decorations used.

Furniture in **Ancient Greece** must not have been very different from furniture in Egypt, as far as the decorative techniques used. The furniture used by the upper classes was lavishly decorated with ivory, precious stones, and gold leaf.

Etruscan furniture was simple, commonly decorated with metal elements. The elaborate fabric that covered the pieces was their primary decoration.

During the **Roman Empire**, furniture belonging to the wealthy classes was richly decorated with marble and various metals. Gold, ivory, and shell inlay was used for decorating lavish beds. Boxes used for storing valuables were covered with metal. Some tables were covered with pieces of marble arranged in mosaic patterns (like marquetry) or with sheet bronze. Others had tops made of rare woods, supported on a base covered with marble or metal pieces, and still others were made completely of these materials.

▼ Granadine nazarí chest, 15th century. Spain. The entire surface of the chest is covered with inlaid decoration.

The Middle Ages

The earliest pieces of furniture that exist in any number date to the Middle Ages and are typically storage or seating pieces. During the **Romanesque** period, furniture was constructed from thick planks held together with large pegged joints, which made them heavy. The decorative design typical of this period was carved geometric and painted motifs, which helped decorate the heavy wood planks and hide joinery and construction elements.

With the change in furniture construction methods that came during the **Gothic** period, the decorative motifs underwent great changes. The artisans were able to obtain thinner boards (and more of them), which favored the use of elaborate joinery and eliminated the need for heavy reinforcement at the joints. It is during this period that the various craft guilds established the first guidelines regarding the use and elaboration of the materials. Decoration was based on the use of architectural motifs like finials, molding, arches, and linen folds, among others. Carved and gilded finials and fretwork were applied to painted furniture. To make the gold stand out, the latter was commonly placed over dark painted paper. The Iberian Peninsula inherited the inlay technique (also known as intarsia), which was applied to furniture until the seventeenth century, from the mudejar tradition. In documents from the thirteenth century, the tarsia technique appears, which is another type of inlay that became popular in the fifteenth century in the regions of Lombardy and Veneto and that involves inserting geometric tessera made of wood, bone, metal or mother of pearl into the wood base. The Italian chests with carved and painted representations of court themes were decorated with a characteristic punching. Carved decorations were also produced leaving the wood plain, with no other decoration than the wood itself.

▶ Detail of the punched decorative motifs along the edge of the boards of a Catalan chest, 15th century. Spain.

▼ Detail of the creative designs of a Catalan Gothic chest, 15th century. The paint has been applied directly to the surface without any preparation coating.

▲ Detail of a drawer of the chest on the left, where the intricate work of inlay marquetry can be seen.

The Renaissance

The Renaissance bloomed in Italy during the **fifteenth century**, creating a style of furniture based on proportions and the consistency of volumes. New types of furniture—including the table and the bed—appeared during this period. Decoration also shared the classical spirit that dominated the Renaissance. The best example, without a doubt, was the use of marquetry to produce trompe l'oeil—landscapes and still life in perspective. Furniture was transformed by the use of decoration, and the techniques used became more diverse: gilding, painting, pyrography, and punching (in chests). The materials used which were different from the ones used until then (for example, fragments of mirrors), also became more diverse. Many furniture pieces were decorated during this period with a technique called *pastiglia*, which is halfway between sculpture and gilding. It involves applying a mixture of plaster, marble powder, and egg over a cloth already attached to wood and molding and then gilding motifs in relief.

During the **sixteenth century**, furniture lost the sense of proportion of the previous period, and its surfaces were decorated with exaggerated architectural elements, giving it a sense of movement and contrast (chiaroscuro). Ornamental moldings, columns, and entablatures were used and were embellished with gilding and painted decoration.

▲ Detail of the lid of an Italian chest, 16th century. The decoration, which resembles paint, was done using pyrography.

▲ Small reliquary from northern Italy, 16th century. It is decorated with printed paper that was colored afterward. This type of decoration is called *Arte Povera*.

◄ Candelabra, 17th century. The wood has a base coat, which is visible in the areas where the paint is missing.

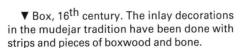

▼ Box, 16th century. The inlay decorations in the mudejar tradition have been done with strips and pieces of boxwood and bone.

The Baroque

New types of furniture appeared during this period, including the console table, the chest of drawers, and the *canterano*. Furniture lost its stiff formality, adopting architectural solutions for decoration, in a search for almost scenographic effects. There was a taste for completely gilded surfaces, and thanks to the trade with tropical countries, ebony and other exotic hardwoods and veneers became available for use. The latter were used to construct and decorate the surfaces of select furniture. Inlaying stones in ebony furniture and combining ebony marquetry with ivory and other woods were some of the most widely used decorative techniques.

The **Louis XIV** style reached its pinnacle with the work of André-Charles Boulle. Boulle was the first cabinetmaker to be universally known for his work for the king, the royal family, and the aristocracy. The marquetry of Boulle was the result of a perfected technique that had already been used in Italy since the sixteenth century. It involved using similar elements in a contrasting manner. For example, one motif was done in bronze over tortoise shell on one side, and the same motif was done with tortoise shell on bronze on the other.

The English **William and Mary** style combined the influence of the Dutch decorative techniques with the repertoire of the Louis XIV style. The most widely used decoration was the floral and garland motifs in exotic and European wood veneers.

▼ Detail of the interior of a Spanish *bargueño*, 17th century. The decoration consists of pieces of inlaid ivory that were later painted and of gilded wood and small ivory columns.

The Eighteenth Century

In the eighteenth century, the style established during the Baroque period became highly exaggerated in the rococo. Decoration was elaborate, profusely gilded, and painted.

In the mid-eighteenth century lacquer became fashionable, although furniture decorated with this technique had already begun to be imported in the previous century. Lacquer is a waterproof varnish that comes from the sap of the lac tree, which is native to China and Japan. It is a gray-colored liquid that can be tinted and that hardens when it comes in contact with air. It is applied in several layers, which when dry become hard and shiny. Shellac was imitated in Europe: In England, Chippendale used a shellac called Japan. In France, the king's official shellac experts created a varnish bearing his name, Martin, while in Venice, Italy, the resin from the juniper tree was used.

The taste for the Baroque faded with the popularity of **Louis XV** style. The type of dresser that is known today appeared. Decoration consisted of veneers and marquetry in exotic woods and applications of gilded bronze elements and lacquer panels.

The **Chippendale** style took its name from the English cabinetmaker Thomas Chippendale. His furniture was known for its use of solid mahogany and satinwood. Unlike French furniture, no gilt bronze was used. Painting and gilding were the predominant techniques.

▲ Detail of a French desk from the last part of the 18th century. The polychrome and patina of the finish try to imitate lacquered furniture.

▲ French dresser from the first part of the 18th century. The veneer is ebony and rosewood.

◀ Popular chair back in the Louis XV style, 18th century. The polychrome and gilding highlight the carved details.

▼ Detail of an oriental trunk painted with mineral pigments over a thick base coat.

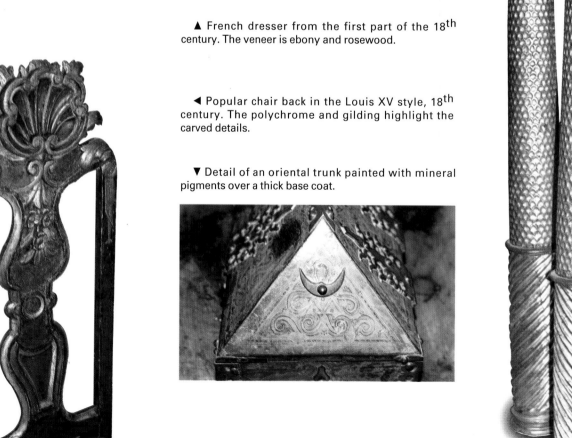

▲ Gilded mirror, 18th century.

▼ A pair of gilded altarpiece columns, 18th century. The capitols are decorated with polychrome gilding.

The Nineteenth Century

The nineteenth century (together with the twentieth century) was without a doubt a period of great and rapid change in furniture and its decoration. In Europe, furniture began to be mass produced, which required specific decorative solutions.

The **neoclassic** style attempted a return to classic forms, resulting in light furniture, decorated with metal ornaments inspired by the French tradition, as well as painting and marquetry of pictorial scenery. Dark wood veneers were combined with carved gilded details.

In France, the **Louis XVI** style adapted the neoclassic taste, reducing the dimensions of the furniture. Mahogany, typically the only wood used, was left visible, and fewer bronze accessories decorated it. Marquetry with gilded elements was also popular.

The **Empire** style developed in France, coinciding with the reign of Napoleon. The decoration was similar to the neoclassic style, but featured more gilded bronze motifs.

The **neo-Gothic** and **historicist** styles were reflections of midcentury thought, and this was visible in the furniture. They advocated a return to the Middle Ages, which was seen as the period of greatest splendor, in opposition to the prevailing classicist style. The decoration stemmed from a reinterpretation of medieval architecture, in which

► French tabletop writing desk, heavily decorated with marquetry in the Boulle style, 18th century. This one is done with pieces of ivory, zinc, wood, and mother of pearl.

periods and styles are mixed. The decorative techniques were not substantially different from previous ones.

Modernism was the last grand style that influenced all of Europe. It was known by different names according to the countries: *Art Nouveau* in France and Belgium, *Modern Style* in England, *Jugendstil* in Germany, and *Modernismo* in Spain, Portugal, and especially Catalonia. This movement was especially influential in the major art forms—such as painting, sculpture, literature, and architecture—and also in the minor ones

—such as mosaic, ceramics, cabinetmaking, textile, glass, and metalwork. However the label *movement* is incorrect. The reality is that some copied certain aspects of the others, so furniture was decorated in innovative ways, but traditional materials were used. For example, modernist furniture was painted and covered with glass; veneers were used along with mosaics; marquetry was done in wood, glass, and ceramic, among other materials; and metals went from being mere decorative accents to becoming an integral part of the piece of furniture.

► French chest, end of the 19th century. The drawers are lacquered and framed with veneered wood. The rest of the chest is veneered.

Materials *and Tools*

*I*n this chapter, all the materials and tools needed for the different techniques used in decorating wood are grouped according to the decorative process and are described. In each section, the basic materials and the preparation of the surface is explained first, followed by the tools, utensils, and auxiliary processes. Painted decoration, because of its nature and the various solutions that the different materials offer, involves the greatest number of materials and tools, although some are used only for specific decorative procedures. Gilding does not require as many materials as painting, but the use of certain products—that is, originals versus substitutes—determines, more than in any other technique used, the quality of the work. Pyrography and punching are both simple decorative techniques using tools specifically designed for that task. Although inlay and marquetry require different techniques and processes, they share some basic materials and many secondary tools and materials. Decorating with veneer is like marquetry because the basic material used is the same for both, and the tools are similar. Decoupage, without a doubt, uses some unique basic materials and tools. Finally, staining and bleaching use similar tools and materials for the initial preparation and the application.

In the following pages, the composition and the correct use of each material and tool is explained, exploring in depth their particular traits and offering a general idea of what is needed for each technical process.

PAINTING

Various procedures and techniques can be used for painting wood. Some are traditional and require specific materials; others are modern and use products that are commercially manufactured.

Independently of the creative technique chosen for decorating wood, auxiliary materials and accessories must be used to carry out such tasks as design, application, and finishing, among others. Therefore the list of required products and utensils is extensive.

Preparation of the Base or Primer

Wood is a porous material, which may present a problem when trying to make paint adhere to it. To solve this problem, the wood must be prepared, because it will be the base for the entire decorating technique that will follow. This can be done using traditional methods or modern processes. In either case, the preparation, or priming, consists of applying a first coat over the surface to be decorated to seal the pores of the wood and to make sure that the various coats of paint adhere.

◀ Rabbit skin glue in sheets (a), in granules (b), whiting or chalk (c).

Traditional Priming

This technique involves applying a mixture of hot rabbit skin glue and whiting.

Rabbit Skin Glue
This is a natural glue made by boiling rabbit skins; it can be used after it has been dissolved with hot water. It is sold in sheets, granules, and powder form, depending on the manufacturer and the composition. The mixture for the primer can be of greater or lesser bonding strength, depending on the concentration of rabbit skin glue in the water.

Whiting
This is made of finely ground calcium carbonate. It is an inert pigment that can be tinted and used as a primer or as a medium (increasing the volume) for other pigments. It is given different names, according to the area where the deposits of calcium carbonate or chalk are found: Spanish, Paris, Meudon, or Florence whiting.

Commercial Primers

These are prepared primers made of various materials.

Gesso
This product is made of gypsum, calcium carbonate, or the like in a plastic medium. Its application results in heavily primed surfaces. It is water soluble.

Acrylic Sealer
This is made from a mixture of different acrylic and vinyl compounds, created by synthesizing plastic materials. It dries quickly and is water soluble.

Enamel
This is a paint made with a synthetic oil base that has a smooth, glossy finish. It can be cleaned with paint thinner. Because of its composition, it is referred to as an oil technique.

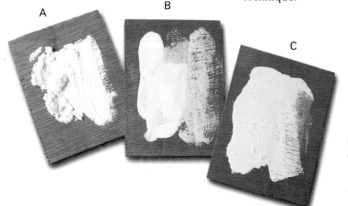

◀ Gesso (a), acrylic sealer (b), white matte enamel (c).

Pigments

A pigment is the colored material that has not been mixed with any medium or binder—that is, it has not been made into paint. Colored paint is formed with a binding vehicle (such as oil, latex, or casein) and a pigment. Pigments can be organic or inorganic, depending on the raw material of its composition. Organic pigments can be natural (derived from vegetables or animals) or synthetic (anilines). Inorganic pigments can be natural (earths) or artificial (oxides).

▲ Pigments in powder form.

Tints

These are colored paints in liquid form that contain soluble pigments. They are used for tinting existing paint, adding color, or varying it without altering its properties. So if a tint is added to a paint that is glossy white and thick, it will continue to have the same properties regarding glossiness and thickness. Tints fade faster than pigments, and their color range is less varied.

Oil Paints

These are paints made from pigments that have linseed oil as a binding vehicle, resulting in a paste of oily consistency. For this reason they are known as oil-based paints, as opposed to paints that are water soluble. Oil paints have different consistencies according to the pigment they contain. Some are thick and opaque, whereas others are transparent and can be used for glazing. Drying, which occurs from the outside in, is quite slow, creating first a hard outer coat and continuing inward. The addition of a cobalt dryer speeds up the drying process for this type of paint.

▼ Oil paints.

◀ Tints.

▼ Pencils.

Color Cards

Decorative paints, regardless of the technique or procedure used, require preliminary planning, which includes choosing the desired color range for the job. Color cards are indispensable for this purpose. Each brand of paint has its own color cards, consisting of an organized catalog of color samples with their corresponding range of tones and hues.

▲ Color cards.

Pencils

After being painted, the wood can be finished using a technique that does not involve paint. Colored pencils are ideal for drawing small details on the paint, for outlining, or for doing designs that require more precision than brushstrokes. There are several types of pencils available specifically designed for each process: oil pencils, watercolor pencils that when brushed with water look like paint, and so on.

Binding Vehicles

These are substances that are mixed with pigments to make paint. The mixture will normally have some kind of soluble vehicle, such as water or mineral spirits. Depending on whether the solvent binds or dissolves the paint, it can be classified as water-based (in which the solvent is water) or oil-based (such as mineral spirits or essence of turpentine)

Water-based Binders

The main water-based binders are latex, casein, and acrylic.

• Latex is a mixture of synthetic resins in water that have a milky appearance. It dries very fast, producing a glossy, transparent finish.

• Casein is a protein from milk that is produced when it curdles and separates from the liquid. It is used in powder form, after being subjected to a process that makes it water soluble. It produces a thick, matte finish.

• Acrylic is a mixture of various acrylic and vinyl components that result from the synthesis of plastic materials. There are two types: those that are soluble in water and those that are soluble in organic solvents. Acrylic paints have a liquid consistency, they dry fast and they do not turn yellow over time, but unlike latex they are not transparent when they dry.

• Beer can also be used as a binder. The paint is prepared by mixing beer with earth pigments—that is, iron oxide, burnt sienna, and light sienna. Once dry, the paint is durable and completely irreversible. This was the procedure traditionally used to paint large surfaces on a budget, imitating wood and its grain.

Oil-based Binders

Linseed oil and varnish are oil-based binders.

• Linseed oil is the liquid obtained from pressing crushed flaxseeds. The highest-quality oil is cold pressed. A variety with more impurities is obtained from a hot pressing. Linseed oil dries slowly (3 to 4 days), from the outside in, first creating a hard outer coat.

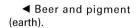

◄ Beer and pigment (earth).

▲ Water-based binders: casein (a), latex (b), acrylic (c).

▲ Oil-based binders: linseed oil (a), matte synthetic varnish (b), enamel (c).

• Varnish can be used as a final protective coat for a painted surface as well as a binding vehicle for pigments. As such it allows color to be applied in thin coats or layers that dry fast, thus making it suitable for glazing.

• Enamel is a commercial paint made of a synthetic or plastic oil-based varnish to which finely crushed pigments have been added. This oil-based paint is used as it comes from the store, so the manufacturer's color cards should be consulted when choosing colors. Tinting it is not advisable. Its finish is smooth and glossy.

The application of the different decorative techniques on a prepared wood surface should be consistent with the rule that oil-based paint should be applied over water-based paint. If the application is done in reverse order, water-based over oil-based, the latter would repel the water-based coat, causing adhesion problems, and the surface would crack in a short period of time.

Modifiers

During the process of painting the wood, it is often necessary to add some materials to the paint, which, without being part of the paint itself, serve to modify the process without changing properties of the paint.

In addition to solvents and dryers, ammonia, a volatile alkaline in a water-based solution, can be used to dissolve casein in particular.

Solvents

Solvents are liquids, which when added to the paint make it more fluid. For water-based products, the solvent is water. Mineral spirits and essence of turpentine are solvents for oil-based paints.

• Essence of turpentine results from the process of purifying the resin of certain conifers. It can be used as a solvent or as a drying agent, because it has a slightly oxidizing property.

• Mineral spirits is a solvent similar to essence of turpentine, but obtained from distilled petroleum.

Dryers

Dryers are emulsions that are used to speed the drying of oil-based paints.

The most commonly used dryer is cobalt dryer, a liquid emulsion of linseed oil and cobalt salts. The latter gives a dark color to the oil; therefore, it is advisable not to use too much of this material, because it would otherwise darken the paint.

▼ Cobalt dryer (a), ammonia (b), mineral spirits (c), essence of turpentine (d).

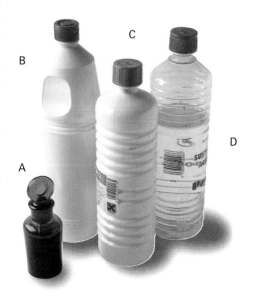

The finish on the painted surface imparts the desired appearance and also helps protect the layer of decorative paint. Therefore, the finish is an integral part of the decorated surface. The materials used to create the finish are varnish and wax.

Varnishes

These are available in liquid or aerosol form. Aerosol varnishes make it possible to achieve a quick, easy, and even finish. For the best results, it is recommended that the varnish be sprayed at a distance of 8 inches (20 cm) from the painted surface. Varnishes are available in oil and water-based mixtures. Liquid varnishes are usually applied with a brush, although one can achieve a finish similar to the one produced with the aerosol by using an atomizer and a little skill. Among the liquid varnishes, two stand out: the water-based acrylics, which are applied over water-based paints and create a surface that is glossy and resistant, and dammar varnishes (a vegetable resin soluble in mineral spirits), which are transparent and light-friendly; and produce a satiny surface.

Waxes

Waxes produce satiny finishes that are deeper than those obtained with varnishes. Like varnish, they are available in various forms (such as liquid, cream, solid, and powder) and with different properties (for example, tinted or with a hardener). Wax is applied with a cotton cloth or strands, and it is hand polished with a rag when dry.

Sanding

Wood must be thoroughly sanded to prepare it for the coat of primer and remove any roughness, any uneven areas, and any type of dirt on its surface. Sanding guarantees that the wood surface will bond perfectly with the primer, which will in turn serve as the base for the paint. Sandpaper is also useful for smoothing and blending the previous layers of paint before the final coat is applied.

It is a good idea to have sandpaper of various grits so the best one for each case can be chosen. The finest ones are labeled 360 or 6, depending on the type, and the coarser ones are 0 or 1, according to the type.

▲ Different types of sandpaper.

Steel Wool and Scouring Pad

These are used for polishing finishes, removing varnish, and creating an antiqued look on patinas. Steel wool is available in rolls or packages and in various grades. Commonly used scouring pads come in different materials and various hardness.

◄ Steel wool (a), fine steel wool (b), scouring pad (c).

▶ Matte varnish in aerosol form for oil-based techniques (a), matte varnish in aerosol for water-based techniques (b), acrylic varnish (c), pure beeswax (d), cream wax (e), dammar varnish (f), atomizer (g).

Auxiliary Supplies

Containers

It is important to have a wide assortment of cans of different shapes and sizes for mixing, storing leftover paint, and cleaning brushes. Food cans and jars are ideal for this purpose.

Solvents, on the other hand, must be stored in their original containers, separately from those that contain mixtures and leftovers. Caution should be observed when pouring any solvent into a plastic container because the solvent can cause the container to dissolve and/or give off toxic substances.

▲ Assortment of containers.

Measuring Utensils

It is necessary to measure and weigh the different materials before mixing a traditional primer, pigments with binding vehicles, and so on. Graduated measuring cups are used to measure the volume of liquids. The glass containers used in laboratories are the most precise; plastic containers, the least precise. A mechanical or electronic scale should be used for measuring solids.

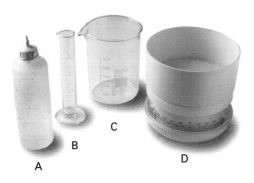

▲ Graduated bottle (a), measuring glass (b), graduated beaker (c), scale (d).

Double Boiler

A double boiler is used for heating a substance slowly and evenly by partially submerging the container that holds it into another one with water.

The traditional preparation of rabbit skin glue is diluted in hot water, and the primer is also applied while hot. Various utensils are needed for these tasks: a burner or an electric heater (never gas because it is dangerous), a wide and low container to hold the water, and a wide-mouthed ceramic pot where the various materials will be diluted. The pot should be made of clay because this material is durable and conserves the heat through the entire application time.

Utensils for Mixing and Kneading

Palette Knife
This consists of a thin, tempered steel blade held with a handle that is normally made of wood. Depending on the form and stiffness of the blade, it can be used for stirring, kneading mixtures, dispensing small quantities of material, or applying decorative paint.

Wooden Spatula
Similar in shape to the palette knife but generally larger, wooden spatulas are used in techniques that do not require great precision and for mixing in processes where solvents or products can react with metal.

Wooden Stick
This is used for briskly stirring mixtures and preparations.

Glass and Wooden Spoons
These are used for spooning, dispensing, mixing, and stirring preparations that react with metal or, in the case of wooden spoons, preparations that require high temperatures.

▼ Palette knives (a), sticks (b), glass spoon (c), wooden spoons (d), wooden spatulas (e).

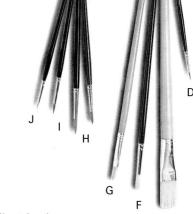

▼ Electric burner, metal pot, and clay pot.

Applicators

There are countless tools for painting wood, many of which are used to create specific decorative results. However, others are used for applying coats of paint, no matter what type of decoration is desired.

Brushes
Brushes can be flat or round. Flat brushes are usually used for applying base coats, priming the wood, or applying liquid varnishes. Round brushes are appropriate for painting corners.

Thin Brushes
Thin brushes, just like regular brushes, are numbered according to the thickness of their tips. There are brushes of different brands, materials, and shapes from which to choose the most appropriate one for a particular task. The brushes most commonly used to apply oil-based paints are those made of bristles, no matter their shape. Brushes made with sable hair are useful for fine finishes and outlining. The best brushes for applying water-based paints are round and made of soft hair—for example, sable, sabeline, or synthetic hair.

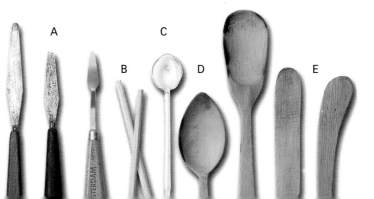

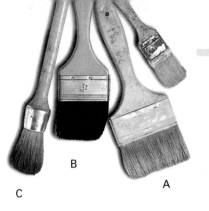

▲ Wide brushes with natural bristles (a), wide brushes with synthetic bristles (b), natural-bristle brush (c). Brushes for oil paints and finishes: brush with sable-hair bristles for lining (d), flat bristles (e), oval made of natural bristles (f), a filbert brush with natural bristles (g). Brushes for water-based techniques: sabeline (h), sable-hair (i), synthetic (j).

Roller

A roller is the most appropriate tool for applications on large surfaces because it produces a smooth, even surface. It is also used to apply the first coats of paint quickly and efficiently.

▲ Roller and tray.

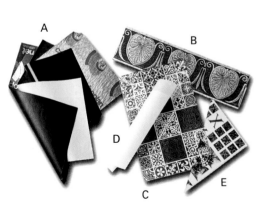

▲ Graphite paper in various colors (a), photocopies on paper (b and c), tracing paper (d), photocopy on acetate (e).

▶ Cutting mat with grid (a), adhesive tape and masking tape (b), scissors and craft knife (c).

Templates and Carbon Paper

A comfortable and easy system for tracing designs to be painted on wood is to use templates and tracing paper. Tracing involves transferring any motif (usually from paper) to a given surface with the help of tracing or graphite paper. A template is a sheet made of any material where the designs that one wishes to transfer onto the surface are cut out. Templates with designs are available ready to use, or they can be personalized and custom made at the shop.

Tracing Paper
This can be used to copy the design directly from a book, print, or other source and to transfer it to the surface using graphite paper.

Graphite Paper
This is for making copies. It is available in various colors, which permits copying on any color surface.

Photocopies on Paper
Black and white photocopies from books with decorative motifs can be copied (using graphite paper) directly onto the surface.

Photocopies on Acetate
Using the same photocopying procedure, a motif can be photocopied on acetate and templates made for stencils.

Adhesive Tape
This is useful for attaching the templates to be traced or for making stencils.

Cutting Mat
This is a soft cutting base with a grid guideline to make clean, straight cuts.

Masking Tape
Masking tape does not leave any marks on the surface. It is used for holding paper in place, protecting areas, and laying out designs for painting.

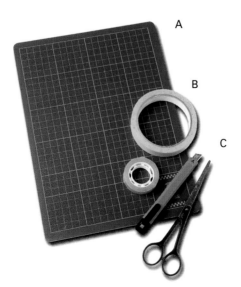

Drawing Tools

Drawing tools are used for creating drawings that can later be transferred to the surface and painted and for transferring existing motifs. The usual measuring tools and a ruler to scale are necessary for transferring designs to scale. Other recommended tools include a wide assortment of pencils of various hardnesses, a compass, markers, and so on.

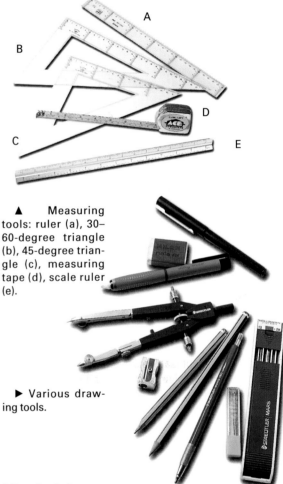

▲ Measuring tools: ruler (a), 30–60-degree triangle (b), 45-degree triangle (c), measuring tape (d), scale ruler (e).

▶ Various drawing tools.

Maulstick

This is an auxiliary tool consisting of a wooden handle (about 5/8 inch [15 mm] thick by 39 inches [1 m] long) with a round piece of cotton wrapped in fabric at one end. It is used as a hand support and provides added security and precision for painting. It is usually held with the left hand tipping the end that has the ball on the paint; the right hand typically rests on it.

▶ Maulstick.

Special Tools for Decorating

Some decorative techniques require specialized tools. Below is a list of them, grouped according to technique.

Marbling

The decorative technique that consists of imitating or recreating the characteristics of marble with paint is called marbling. The creation of marbling effects on wood requires the use of specific tools to produce the characteristics of the original material, such as veining, spattering, areas of diffused color, and water effects.

Veining Brush
Round brush with long bristles (usually from a badger) for veining.

Toothed Spalter
Flat brush whose ferrule is divided to form several points, from which some long bristles stand out. It is used for creating water effects.

Diffuser
Consists of a handle that supports a cylindrical head made of rubber or foam. It is used to diffuse the veins.

Mixer
Flat brush with short hairs (usually from a badger) that is used to smooth out the veins.

Long-haired Brush
Flat brush with long hair that can be used to create the appearance of texture with paint, using a combing process.

Veining

This is a decorative technique for the application of a series of water effects or veins on the surface of paint that is still wet. Some types of veining require the removal of material.

Veining Tool
Plastic implement with a grooved surface that produces the veins when passed over wet paint.

Comb
This consists of a wooden or plastic handle with long teeth that remove part of the fresh paint to produce waves and lines.

Toothed Scraper
A scraper with teeth that produces an effect similar to the comb.

Scrapers
These are used to remove paint as well as to apply thick layers of paint.

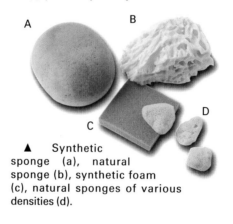

▲ Synthetic sponge (a), natural sponge (b), synthetic foam (c), natural sponges of various densities (d).

Sponging

A characteristic sponging effect can be achieved by using the sponge over a layer of paint or by applying paint directly to the surface. The effects vary depending on the type of sponge used.

Natural Sponge
Natural sponges are resistant to solvents, they do not fall apart, and they are durable. It is a good idea to have several pieces of various densities or designs.

Artificial Sponge
Artificial sponges are made with synthetic plastic. They are usually dense, so they absorb a lot of paint. However, they are hard to clean, and they are not as durable as natural ones.

The performance of commercial foams is similar to these sponges, but sponges make different decorative patterns, depending on their density, pore arrangement, and design.

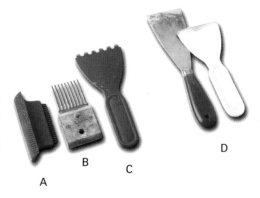

▲ Veining tool (a), comb (b), toothed scraper (c), scrapers (d).

Stamping

Stamping is a technique used for making a design on a surface using a template. Templates, also called stamps, can be purchased ready to use and in many varieties, or they can be made at home.

To make a template, the following are needed:

Sheet of Extruded Polyurethane
This inexpensive and easy-to-work material is used for cutting out the desired design. Its commercial name is Styrofoam.

Eraser
This can be used instead of polyurethane when the chosen designs are small or require great detail.

Scalpel
This can be used to cut the material with greater precision.

Sheet of Wood
This makes a good base for the template and allows easy manipulation.

Handle
A handle is not always needed, but it makes the stamping process much easier.

Glue
Polyvinyl acetate (PVA) adhesive is used to bond the template to the base and the base to the handle.

▼ Commercial stamps (a), extruded polyurethane (b), wood (c), scalpel and eraser (d), handle (e), glue (f).

◀ Veining brush (a), toothed spalter (b), diffuser (c), mixer (d), long-haired brush (e).

G ilding techniques and those derived from it, require specific materials and tools. The term gilding, in addition to referring to the covering of a surface with gold or gold-colored metals, also describes by association the covering with other metals, such as silver and copper. Unlike with the other techniques included in this book, with gilding, the use of certain materials directly influences the quality of the results. Without a doubt, the result of a gilding project that has been carried out with traditional materials will be far superior to one that has been carried out with modern ones, even when traditional processes are imitated.

Basic Materials

The basic materials for gilding are, obviously, the gold and silver leaf or leaf of various alloys. There are also many substitutes to choose from, depending on the desired results.

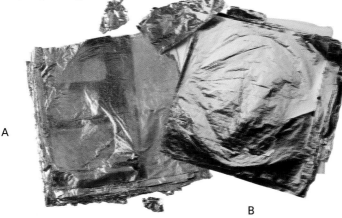

▲ Gold leaf (a), silver leaf (b).

Gold and Silver Leaf

Fine gold and silver used for gilding are sold in sheets called leaves. These sheets are thin (the gold sheets may even be thin enough to see through), available in sizes that range from 3×3 inches (8×8 cm) to 6×6 inches (16×16 cm), depending on the metal, and they are sold in booklets with thin paper pages between which the leaves are inserted. The most common size is 4×4 inches (10×10 cm). Gold and silver leaves are extremely delicate, they wrinkle easily, and they can blow away because they are so thin.

Gold and Silver Substitutes

Because of the difficulty of gilding with gold and silver leaves and the high cost of pure gold, sometimes they are replaced with other materials that are easier to apply and cost less.

Enamel
Commercial gold or silver paint similar to enamel has a smooth, glossy finish.
Watercolor
Paint in the color of gold, silver, or other metal that comes in cake form and dissolves in water.
Pastel
The color is applied directly to the surface with the bars of pastel in metallic tones.
Powder
Gold substitutes or imitations also come in powdered form. Lacquer is used as a binder.
Oil
Oil paints come in a wide range of tones that can be used to imitate antique metals.

▶ Gold enamel (a), silver wash (b), silver watercolor (c), imitation gold powder (d), copper powder (e), gold pastel in bar form (f), antique gold oil paint (g).

Preparation of the Surface

Priming

All wood surfaces require preparation before gilding. Such priming consists of a hot mixture of diluted rabbit skin glue and whiting, which is applied in layers while hot, using a brush.

Rabbit Skin Glue
Organic glue made from boiling rabbit skins. It is sold in sheets, granules, or powder form (see page 16).
Whiting
Calcium carbonate, an inert pigment made of fine particles. It is known as chalk, Spanish, Paris, Meudon, or Florence whiting.

▲ Rabbit skin glue in granules (a), whiting (b).

Adhesives and Binders

Once the surface has been properly prepared, the materials that serve as the base for the metal leaf and hold it in place are applied.

Bole
Bole, also known as Armenian bole, is used as the base for the gold leaf. It is applied over the primer to act as a flexible "cushion," which creates the proper base and allows the gold to be polished without breaking. It is a mixture of iron oxide, clay, and calcium and magnesium silicates in various proportions; the colors range from ochre to bright red. Red bole is normally used for gold leaf, whereas ochre bole is used for silver leaf. Acrylic paints or gouache in colors similar to the ones previously indicated can be used as substitutes for bole.
Size
Size is a water-based varnish that is used as an adhesive for modern water gilding. The metal is applied when it is mordant, before it dries out completely, and when it is still tacky.
Mixtion
Mixtion is an oily varnish made of linseed oil plus some other additive, used in the oil-based gilding technique. Mixtion has a mordant period of about 12 hours. To find out when it is in perfect condition for gilding, one simply needs to rub a finger on the surface: The finger should not stick but a characteristic sound is made.

In the relievo technique, tempera paint is used to cover the gilded layer on the surface. Various pigments and a binder, which can be egg or gum arabic, are used to make the tempera.
Gum Arabic
Gum arabic is the product of different species of African acacias. It is sold in large, translucent pieces of a yellowish color. It is water soluble.

◀ Red bole (a), ochre bole (b), red gouache (c), size (d), mixtion (e). Tempera paint binders: gum arabic (f), egg (g).

Pigments

The relievo technique involves covering the gilded surface with a layer of egg tempera paint. Once dry, it is removed in certain areas with toothpicks or other tools, exposing parts of the gold layer. Pigments are used to make the tempera paint.

▲ Powdered pigments.

Shellac

Shellac is an alcohol-soluble animal resin that is sold in flakes. To prepare it, 7 ounces (200 g) of lacquer are diluted in 1 quart (1 liter) of alcohol, and the mixture is filtered through a piece of thin cloth with an open weave. The preparation should be stored in a glass jar with a tight lid. The shellac is used to apply the protective, finishing layer to the gold.

▼ Prepared shellac (a), shellac in flakes (b), alcohol (c).

Petroleum Jelly and Talcum

The person doing the gilding should apply talcum powder to his or her hands to prevent the fragile gold leaf, or pieces of it, from sticking to the skin. The petroleum jelly is used to dampen the gilder's tip.

▲ Liquid petroleum jelly (a), talcum powder (b).

▶ Asphalt (a), turpentine (b).

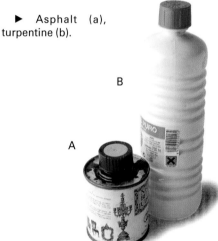

Asphalt

Asphalt diluted in turpentine is used to create the look of aged patina on the gold. It is a mixture of natural hydrocarbons with a consistency that is between liquid and solid, and it is soluble in oils and spirits (turpentine). It gives it a warm, dark brown color and can be used to achieve the characteristic glazing effect.

Gilder's Pad

This tool is used for holding and cutting the gold leaf during the gilding process. Various materials are needed to make a gilder's pad:

Wood
A rectangular piece of wood about 6 × 9 × 1/2 inches (15 × 22 × 1 cm). This serves as the base of the pad.

Felt
A thick piece of this material is placed over the wood.

Chamois
This is used for covering the wood and the felt. The gold leaf is laid on it.

Parchment Paper
This should be attached to one side of the pad to prevent drafts that could cause the gold leaf to blow away.

Stapler
This is used to attach the felt and chamois.

Gimp
This is used to finish the edges.

Tacks and Hammer
These are used to attach the gimp to the edges.

▼ Chamois (a), parchment paper (b), wood chipboard (c), tacks (d), felt and gimp (e), stapler (f), and hammer (g).

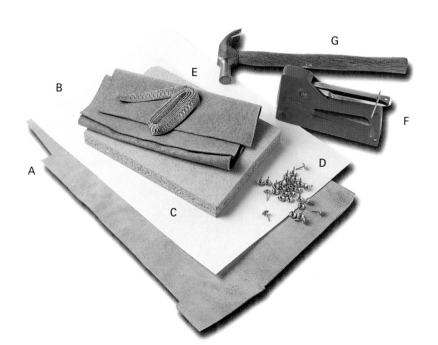

Measuring Tools

Accurate measuring or weighing is necessary for preparing the wood and for mixing the liquid shellac.

Graduated containers are used for measuring liquids. The most accurate are the glass ones found in laboratories. A scale should be used for solids.

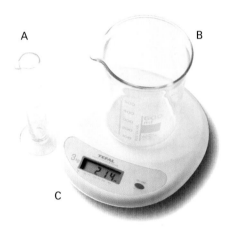

▲ Measuring cylinder (a), beaker (b), electronic scale (c).

Double Boiler

As explained in the previous chapter, a double boiler is used for heating something slowly by partially submerging the container that holds it inside another one with water, which in turn is heated on a burner. Wood surfaces are prepared by applying a mixture of rabbit skin glue and whiting heated in a double boiler. The tools required for this are a burner or an electric hot plate, a container that is wide and low for holding the water, and a wide-mouthed ceramic container for heating the various materials.

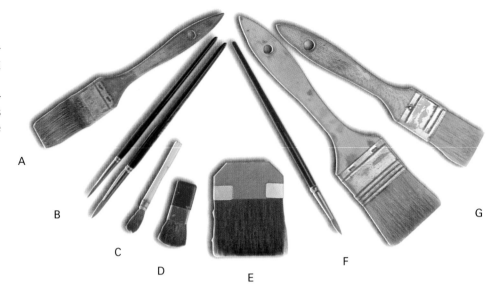

▲ Bristle brush (a), round sabeline brushes (b), ox-hair mop (c), synthetic brush (d), camel-hair gilder's tip (e), round sable-hair brush (f), bristle brushes (g).

▲ Spatula (a), spoons (b).

Mixing Utensils

Various utensils are needed for manipulating and mixing the products. Several wooden spoons and spatulas, as well as a spoon made of glass or any other material that is not metal, are the most useful.

Applicators

The gilding technique requires the use of various applicators with specific functions.

Wide Brush
This is a rectangular brush that is used for applying primer to the surface that is to be gilded and for applying asphalt and shellac finishes.

Sabeline Brush
This is used for applying bole and shellac.

Ox-Hair Mop
This is a spherical brush that is used to place, brush, and remove the small fragments of gold leaf that have not adhered to the surface.

Gilder's Tip
A flat brush made of a row of straight and even hairs held between two pieces of cardboard. It is used for picking up the gold leaf and for applying it onto the surface to be gilded.

Sabeline-Hair Brush
This is the most appropriate brush for applying the layer of tempera over the gilded surface in the relievo technique.

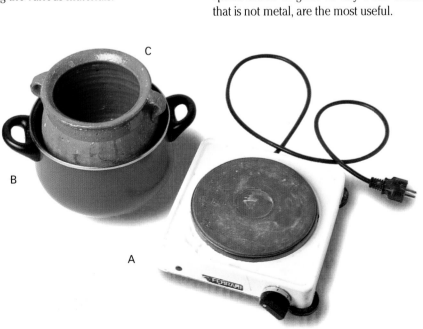

◄ Electric hot plate (a), container for water (b), clay pot (c).

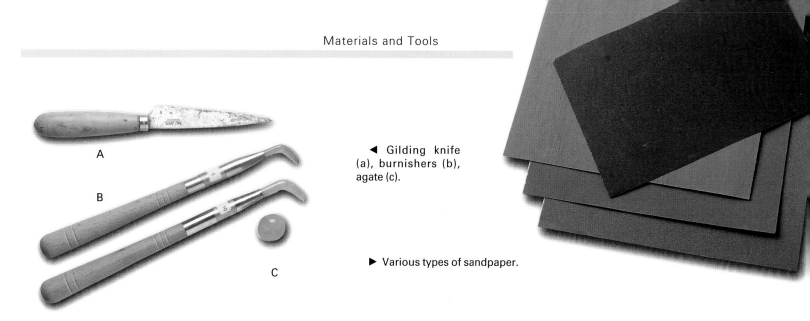

◄ Gilding knife (a), burnishers (b), agate (c).

► Various types of sandpaper.

Tools for Cutting and Burnishing

Gilding Knife
This is a tool with a long and narrow blade and a wood handle. It looks like a common knife but without a cutting edge. It is used for cutting and smoothing the gold leaf.

Burnisher
This is used for burnishing gold or silver leaf. It consists of a hard, smooth, rounded stone attached to a wood handle. Agate is the most common stone, but any other type can be used. The fangs of carnivorous animals were used in the old days.

▼ Tracing paper (a), photocopy on paper (b), photocopy on tracing paper (c), tracing papers (d).

Templates and Tracings

Templates and tracings are the easiest and most comfortable way to transfer the motifs to the paint when using the relievo technique. Any design (usually on paper) can be traced to a surface by using graphite paper or tracing paper.

Tracing Paper
This is paper for copying and transferring a motif directly from a book, print, or other source to a given surface.

Graphite Paper
Graphite paper makes a copy of anything drawn on it. It is sold in various colors, which allows copies to be made on different colored surfaces.

Photocopies
These are made on either regular or tracing paper, and are convenient for tracing designs directly onto a surface.

Sandpaper

The surface of the wood must be sanded thoroughly to prepare it for the base coat and eliminate any roughness, uneven areas, or imperfections. The various layers of the preparation are also sanded, to make sure the base is in perfect condition for priming.

It is important to have sandpaper of various grits so that the most appropriate one can be used in each case.

Drawing Tools and Toothpicks

These tools are used for the relievo technique. The drawing tools are used for creating designs that are later transferred to the surface. The toothpicks are used to scratch and remove the paint where necessary to form the desired decorative motif. Simple kitchen toothpicks can be used, or boxwood sticks, which are especially made for the relievo technique.

▼ Various drawing tools (a), boxwood stick (b), common toothpicks (c).

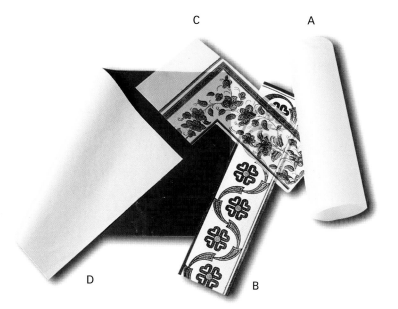

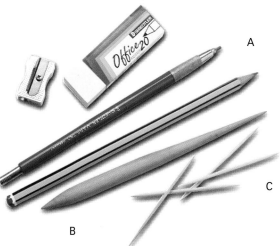

PYROGRAPHY AND PUNCHING

*P*yrography is a traditional decorative technique that is still widely used today. The technique consists of darkening or blackening the surface of the wood by applying controlled heat to it. This procedure produces designs that almost have a painted look. The punching technique is used to create designs and relief effects on the surface of the wood. A punch is tapped with a hammer or mallet to mark the wood, which will create the desired motif in relief. Although these two techniques are different, their common trait is that, unlike other decorative techniques, no added material is needed. The surface may look different, but its essence has not been changed.

Tools

Wood-burning Iron

This is an electric tool, which includes a transformer and a handle with replaceable tips. The transformer is connected directly to the current. There is a wide range of brands and models available, but the most efficient are the ones that have a temperature regulator.

The electric soldering irons whose handles have been modified to accommodate replaceable points are appropriate for work that is not detailed or surfaces that are not large. They are also an inexpensive alternative to the conventional wood-burning iron.

Cleaning the Pyrography Design

When the pyrography work is finished, the residue that is caused from burning the surface of the wood must be eliminated. Clean paint brushes and other soft brushes are used to remove the ash residue. A fine-grit sandpaper is useful for blending, lightening, or eliminating parts of the design.

Punches

Punches are small steel bars with a relief design on one end. They are used by tapping on the opposite end with a nylon head hammer.

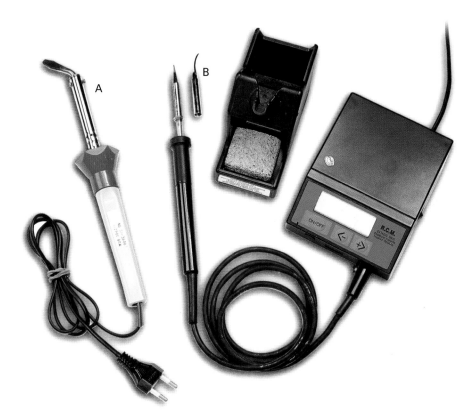

▲ Soldering iron (a), wood-burning iron (b).

▶ Sheets of sandpaper, different types of brushes.

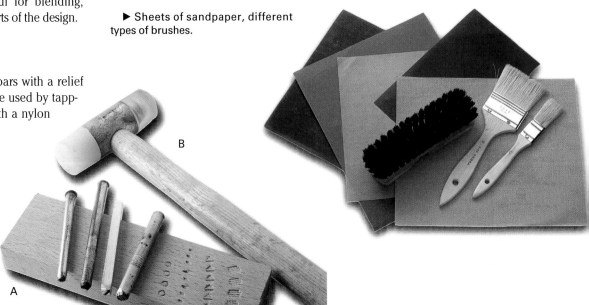

▶ Punches (a), nylon head hammer (b).

Preparing the Surface

The preparation of the wood of both processes involves a thorough sanding to eliminate uneven areas, raised grain, and unwanted particles. It is important that the surface be perfectly smooth and polished. For this purpose, 150-grit sandpaper is used, which can be fitted to a block of wood to apply even pressure when sanding.

▲ Sandpaper and blocks.

Design

Both techniques require a design before the decoration can be applied. The design should be well defined; it is advisable not to leave anything to chance. Various drawing tools are required to carry out the decorating project and to create one's own design, whether drawing straight lines, complex geometric motifs, or curved shapes. The paper with the design is laid on top of the surface to transfer it to the wood. Then the design is traced, pressing hard with the pencil while following the outline. It is also possible to copy existing designs directly onto tracing paper.

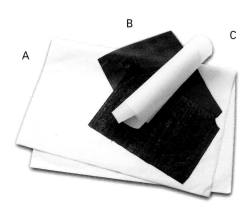

▲ Drawing tools.

◀ Thin paper (a), graphite paper (b), tracing paper (c).

▼ Book of decorative designs.

Finishes

The finish on the burned wood surface must completely protect the wood and be durable. Therefore the best finish is achieved by first applying a wood filler and sanding it after it dries (with steel wool and sandpaper), applying a coat of wax, and then polishing it with a cotton cloth. The filler is toxic, so it is necessary to wear a respirator and neoprene gloves while applying it.

Punched wood, on the other hand, does not require a highly protective finish. Simply applying a coat of wax over it is sufficient. The wax is applied with cotton strands, and it is buffed by rubbing briskly with a clean cotton cloth when it is dry.

▼ Number 0000 fine steel wool (a), 400-grit sandpaper (b), wood block (c).

▼ Wood filler (a), respirator (b), neoprene gloves (c).

▼ Wax.

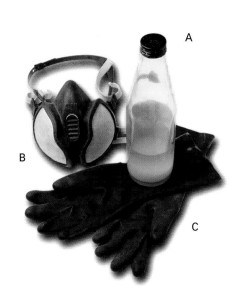

INLAY AND MARQUETRY

*T*he techniques of inlay and marquetry are different from each other, but there is a tendency to confuse them and to consider them the same. Marquetry involves decorating the surface of the wood by gluing fragments of wood veneers or other materials to it, creating a smooth surface. Inlay, on the other hand, is the decoration of a solid board by inserting pieces of wood, metal, bone, or other materials in incisions that had been made in the surface.

They are two very different technical processes but they share certain materials and quite a few tools.

Basic Materials

Backing Boards

According to the definition of *inlay* above, the backing material for this technique can only be solid wood. However, marquetry can be done on solid wood (normally of low quality) and on manufactured board—that is, made in a factory following one of several processes.

Chipboard
Chipboard is made by bonding wood chips mixed with synthetic resins under pressure.

Fiberboard
These boards are made of wood fibers bonded with synthetic resins and formed under high pressure.

Plywood
Plywood boards are made from thin sheets of wood, stacked and glued with the grain of one layer perpendicular to that of the next layer.

Laminated Wood
These boards are made of several pieces of solid wood aligned and glued to each other.

Inlay Wood

These are pieces of wood that range from $5/32$ to $3/8$ inch (4 to 10 mm) thick, come in various sizes, and are used for inlay work. Those of medium thickness, about $3/16$ inch (5 mm), are the most widely used. They can be purchased or made in the shop with remnants or leftover pieces of solid wood.

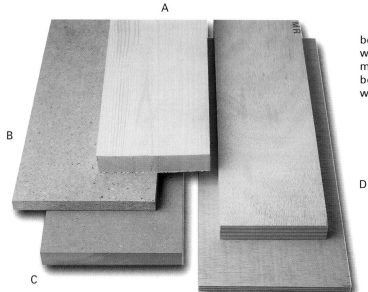

◀ Factory-made boards: laminated solid wood (a), chipboard (b), medium-density fiberboard (MDF) (c), plywood (d).

◀ Inlay boards (a), solid hardwood (b).

Veneers

Veneers are thin sheets of wood whose thickness ranges between $1/64$ and $1/32$ inch (0.4 and 0.8 mm). They vary in size, and they are made for use in marquetry. The sheets are sold unfinished or colored with dyes (see the chapter on "Veneering").

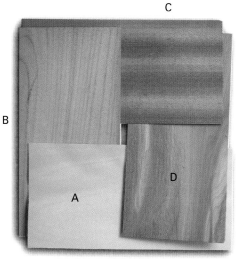

▶ Beech *Fagus sylvatica* (a), Cherry *Prunus avium* (b), Embero *Lovoa trichilioides* (c), Virginia Cedar *Juniperus virginiana* (d).

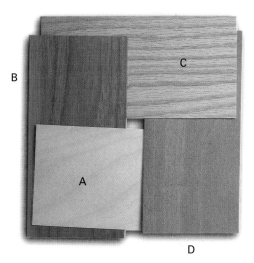

▲ Birch *Betula* (a), American walnut *Juglan nigra* (b), Red oak *Querqus rubra* (c), Plantain *Platanus acerifolia* (d).

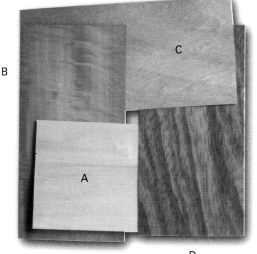

◀ Poplar *Populus* (a), Eucalyptus *Eucalyptus globulus* (b), Okume *Aucoumea klaineana* (c), Etimoe *Coapifera salikounda* (d).

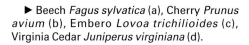

▼ Sapele *Entandrophragma cilindricum* (a), Sycamore *Acer* (b), African cedar *Guarea cedrata* (c), Iroco *Chlorophola excelsa* (d).

▼ Sequoia *Sequoia sempervirens* (a), Ash *Fraxinus excelsior* (b), Mukale *Gambeya africana* (c), Chestnut *Castanea sativa* (d).

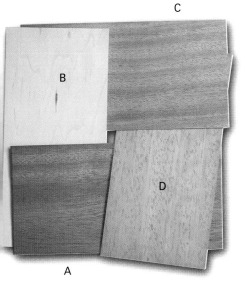

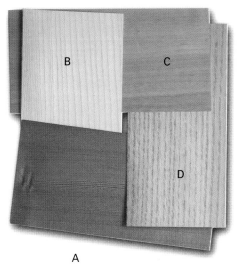

Commercial Pieces

It is possible to purchase ready-to-use pieces for marquetry or inlay. Boxwood strips and strips of other types of wood stained black to imitate ebony are used mainly for inlay projects; in marquetry they are only used to frame or to edge certain motifs. In the latter case, mainly borders and premade designs are used; however, these are rarely used for inlay projects.

▲ Strips and bandings for marquetry.

▲ Commercial marquetry motifs.

Traditional Materials

Traditionally, many different natural materials other than wood have been used for the marquetry and inlay techniques.

Brass and zinc, in sheets and strips, are good examples. Boxwood in sheets or strips, bone and ivory in sheets or small pieces, together with mother of pearl in sheets or pieces and ebony in pieces are preferred for use in inlay.

Elephant hunting and the subsequent ivory trade have been banned for years. Today, old ivory is used for inlay and marquetry projects. It is found in many objects, like letter openers, billiard balls, and piano keys, among others. It is recommended to purchase more than is needed and to store it appropriately, because this material is difficult to find and its use is more and more restricted.

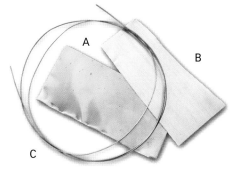

▲ Brass sheet (a), zinc sheet (b), brass strip (c).

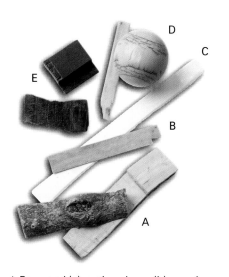

▲ Boxwood (a), antique bone (b), new bone (c), ivory (d), ebony (e).

▲ Mother of pearl.

Adhesives

Of the many types of adhesives that can be used for either of the two techniques, the preferred ones are those that can be reversed. The instant adhesive glues produce a fast-acting bond, but they do not allow any later modifications. The most appropriate glues are rabbit skin, fish, and bone glues (natural) and white carpenter's glue (synthetic).

Liquid Fish Glue

This adhesive is prepared to be used cold. Its drying time is 8 hours.

Rabbit Skin and Bone Glue

These are animal-derived glues made from boiling the skins of rabbits or animal bones and cartilage. They are sold in sheets, granules, or powder form. They require a laborious preparation, which involves soaking and dissolving them in a double boiler (see the chapter on "Veneering").

Polyvinyl Acetate Glue (PVA)

This is also called carpenter's glue. It is a polyvinyl acetate soluble in water, which becomes transparent once it is dry. The residue is easy to remove, and it does not stain. Its drying time is about 24 hours.

▲ Liquid fish glue (a), bone glue in sheet form (b, c), rabbit skin glue in sheet form (d), PVA glue (e), bone glue in granules (f).

Assembling and Support Materials

Adhesive tapes are used as assembly materials in marquetry. They are used to hold together the sheets that form the marquetry before they are glued and to hold them in place during the gluing and drying process. A thin, adhesive tape made specially for marquetry is used for this purpose; it is made with a weak adhesive that is easy to remove. Masking tape and gummed tape, used by painters, are also common. A thick sheet of paper is glued over a veneer sheet to reinforce it, to make the cutting process easier and to avoid breaking the pieces by accident. The paper is also useful for assembling pieces when dealing with large marquetry projects.

Sanding Materials

When the inlay process is completed, after the glue is dry, the surface is smoothed—first with a plane and then with a thorough sanding. Sanding is also used for polishing and smoothing the pieces that are inlaid in the wood. Therefore it is important to have different grades of sandpaper, as well as a block to sand with to apply even pressure. This block can be a piece of wood, cork, or foam to which the sandpaper is attached.

Finishes

The finish acts as a protective coat and highlights the completed work. A final layer of wax, which is applied using cotton strands or a cloth, is a good idea for marquetry and inlay jobs. When dry, the surface is polished with a clean cotton cloth. Wax is a compound of animal, vegetable, or mineral substances that are mixed with a solvent to turn them into an oily solid. Way gives the wood a beautiful satiny finish.

▲ Sandpaper and block.

▼ Wax and cotton strands.

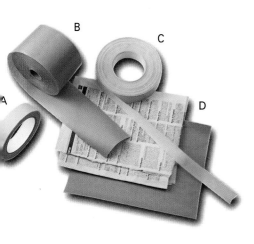

▲ Masking tape (a), gummed paper (b), marquetry tape (c), reinforcement papers (d).

Tools for Measuring, Checking, and Marking

Measure

There are several versions of this measuring tool: They can be made of wood, plastic, aluminum or other metal, or fabric tapes rolled inside a metal casing.

Ruler

This is a smooth-edged strip used to draw straight lines and to check flat surfaces. It can be made of wood, plastic, or metal, the latter being preferred for its durability.

Try Square

The try square consists of two uneven arms set at a right angle. It is used to check right angles accurately and to draw lines perpendicular to a given edge.

Marking Gauge

This instrument is made of wood and used to mark lines of the desired dimensions parallel to any of the sides of the surface.

Tools for Drawing and Tracing

The designs must be drawn on paper and then transferred to the veneer or other material used for inlay by tracing the drawing with graphite paper under it. Transparent tracing paper makes it easier to copy directly from a drawing, photograph, or print. Designs can also be duplicated from decorative pattern books (see chapter on "Painting").

▼ Tracing paper (a), graphite paper (b).

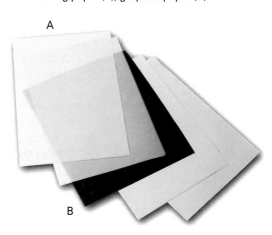

▼ Measuring tape (a), try square (b), folding rule (c), metal ruler (d), marking gauge (e).

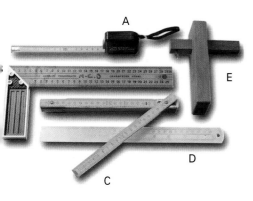

Tools

► Cutting gauge.

▼ Planes.

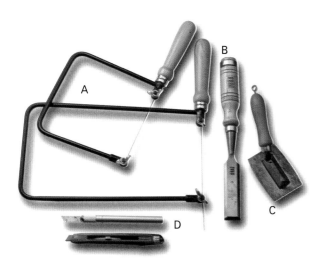

▲ Scroll saws (a), chisel (b), veneer saw (c), knives (d).

▼ Plane with toothed blade, plane with regular blade.

Tools for Cutting, Smoothing, and Polishing

Cutting Gauge

This is used for cutting strips from the veneers or for deeply marking the area that is to be removed from solid wood. It is similar to the marking gauge, but instead of a steel point it has a small cutting blade.

Plane

The plane consists of a wood block 8 to 12 inches (20 to 30 cm) long, with a diagonally slanted opening for inserting a blade at a 45-degree angle, held in place by a wedge. It is used for smoothing and polishing the areas of the inlay material that stand out from the surface.

Toothed-blade Plane

This is used to prepare the surface onto which the marquetry will be attached. The toothed blade, which is set vertically, makes small tracks on the wood to hold the glue, promoting excellent bonding of the veneer.

Fret Saw

This is mainly used for cutting marquetry pieces. It consists of a fine blade mounted vertically into a metal frame. The frames can be of different sizes. There are blades for cutting wood and blades for cutting metal. The most appropriate ones for cutting veneer range from numbers 0 to 3. They should be mounted to cut on the pull—that is, with the teeth on the outside and facing downward.

Chisel

This is used for making hollow areas in the wood and for marking the outline of motifs that are to be cut out as part of the inlay process. It is also used for cutting veneer. It consists of a steel blade with a horizontal cutting edge and a handle that is usually made of wood. Its width varies from 1/8 inch to 1 1/2 inches (4 to 40 mm).

Gouge

This chisel with a carved blade is used for making the hollow cavity in the solid wood where the inlay is inserted. The curved blade is available in different sizes.

Mortise Chisel

This is used during the inlay process for cutting out corners and edges. The mortise chisel has a thicker blade—the width varies from 3/32 inch to 3/4 inch (2 and 20 mm)—but its thickness increases in the same proportion.

Veneer Saw

This consists of a blade about 3/64 or 3/32 inch (1 or 2 mm) thick and 3 to 4 inches (7 to 10 cm) long. It has teeth on both sides and is used for cutting veneer. The cut should always be made from the outside in, perpendicular to the person doing the cutting.

Manual Router Plane

This is used to level large areas of the surface of the board and to make grooves for inserting the inlay. The cut should be made from the outside, pulling toward the body. The tool consists of a metal device with two handles, at the center of which a changeable blade is attached with a screw. The depth of the blade can be adjusted, which allows the cut to be gauged.

Scraper Blade

This is used in marquetry for smoothing and leveling the glued veneer. It has a semi-hard, good-quality tempered blade. The burr along the longer sides of the blade makes the cut. To guarantee a perfect cut, the blades must be polished often. This is done by eliminating the old burr and filing and smoothing the edges on a sharpening stone covered with oil, until they are square. Then, a new cutting edge is created by burnishing the edge at the proper angle.

▼ For corners and edges: mortise chisels (a), gouges (b).

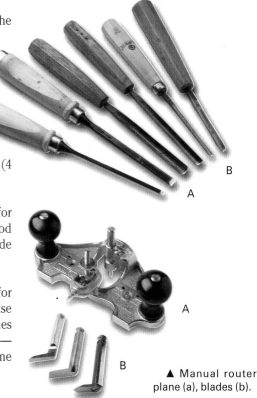

▲ Manual router plane (a), blades (b).

Gimlet

This is a conical screw point with a handle for turning manually. It is used for boring small holes where the scroll saw can be inserted to begin cutting the veneer or the piece that is to be inlaid. The most appropriate sizes for this purpose are numbers 1, 5, and 2.

Awl

This has a fine metal point with a wooden handle. Its use is similar to that of the gimlet. It is also used for picking up (by lightly poking) small marquetry pieces.

Hand Drill

This has a chuck at one end and a fixed handle and a crank that allows rapid drilling at the other.

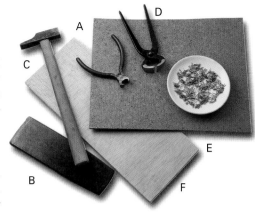

▲ Cork pad (a), steel sheet (b), hammer (c), pincers (d), small nails (e), wooden base (f).

Reinforcing Veneer

As explained before, the veneer sheets used in marquetry are extremely thin. To cut them correctly, a base or packet must be made to give them hardness and rigidity. This is done by bonding the veneer with rabbit skin glue onto a piece of paper and placing the various pieces of veneer, 4 to 8, underneath. The veneer pieces are attached with fine nails to a piece of wood protected with a cork pad. When this process is finished, the packet is separated from the cork, and the heads of the nails are cut off with pincers. Using the steel sheet as a base, the points on the other side are flattened into the veneer by pounding them with a hammer.

Bird's Mouth Jig

The use of a guide is essential for properly holding and cutting the desired design from the veneer with a fret saw. This is made of a sheet of plywood that is about 3/8 inch (8 mm) thick with a V-shape incision that has a 1/4 inch (7 mm) diameter hole at the apex. At the other end, there is a larger hole with a piece of wood nailed across that allows it to be clamped to a table. The V-shape allows the veneer to be cut in every direction.

Clamping Tools

To make sure that the veneer and the inlaid pieces are glued properly and evenly, certain tools are used for holding them in place and for applying pressure to them.

When the pieces have been inserted into the solid wood, they are held in place firmly with clamps. These tools create enough pressure to make sure that the pieces do not come loose. It is a good idea to protect the inlaid and the wood surfaces by placing a sheet of paper and a block of wood between them and the clamp.

For sheets of veneer, the best tool is a bookbinding press to exert an even pressure over the entire surface. If one is not available, it is possible to make one in the shop. Several strips of wood are placed on the table, with another rigid board of the same size on top of them. Two sheets of paper are put on this, and over them another rigid board. Finally, strips of wood like the first ones are placed on top. A clamp is attached to each end of the strips of wood to make sure they stay in place and exert the appropriate pressure.

▲ Scraper blades (a). For sharpening: oil (b), file (c), burnisher (d), sharpening stone (e).

◀ Gimlet (a), awl (b), hand drill (c).

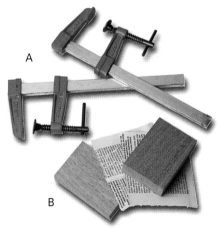

▲ Tools for pressing inlay: clamps (a), pieces of wood and paper (b).

◀ Bird's mouth jig.

▶ Bookbinding press.

Veneering, as its name indicates, involves attaching sheets of wood to a wood surface. One or several sheets of veneer of the same or of different types of wood are bonded to the surface, which can be natural or fabricated, covering it completely. Unlike marquetry, the goal of veneering is not to produce complicated designs. At most, simple geometric designs are achieved with different pieces of the same veneer. The beauty of the decoration is in the characteristics of each piece of wood, whether innate (for example, color, grain, figure, hardness, pores, and so on) or acquired through some coloring or staining process. Veneering gives a rich appearance to a surface of simple quality.

Basic Materials

Veneer

A veneer is a thin sheet of wood ranging from $1/64$ to $1/32$ inch (0.4 to 0.8 mm). The wood destined to the manufacturing of veneer can be cut according to various processes: sawing, rotary cutting, or slicing.

Sawing involves cutting the wood with big, circular saws. This produces pieces of veneer ranging between $3/64$ and $13/64$ inch (1 and 5 mm). However, sawing is not commonly used.

Rotary cutting requires placing the piece of wood in a big, rotating lathe, where the wood is trapped with a bar and where a blade (separated from the bar with a space equal to the thickness of the veneer) cuts a continuous sheet of veneer. This process allows the production of very thin veneer, less than $1/250$ inch (0.1 mm) thick.

Slicing is based on the same principal, but here the wood is cut obliquely, with ascending and descending movements. The resulting veneer has the width of the piece of wood and a thickness that ranges between $1/64$ and $1/16$ inch (0.5 and 1.5 mm).

Different grain configurations of the veneer are created, depending on the cutting process. The veneer is left to dry afterward and then packed and stored according to the order in which it was cut.

▲ Veneer in its natural color and tinted.

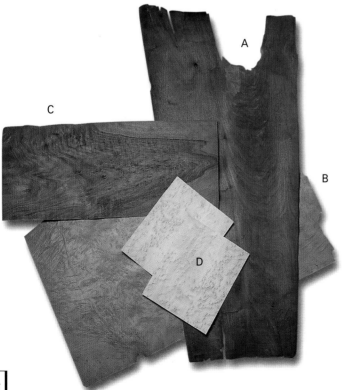

◄ Mahogany crotch (a), maple burl (b), walnut crotch (c), erable butt, also called bird's eye (d).

The part of the tree from which the wood is extracted (butt, burl or knot, trunk or crotch) also determines the type of veneer that is produced. Long veneer sheets are obtained from the **trunk** of the tree, and they generally have wide graining. The veneer extracted from the **burl** has a characteristic design with little circles arranged closely together. Veneer with converging figures is obtained from the **crotch**.

To sum up, the look of a veneer depends on the area of the tree it came from and the type of cut. Stained veneer is also available commercially, so the possibilities are almost endless. Based on the grain, veneer can be flat (with even grain), wavy (with different tones of grain that look like waves), watery (with sinuous waves that produce a moire effect), knotty (with knots surrounded by many radii), or blistered (with sinuous grain and streaks of bright color).

SAWING

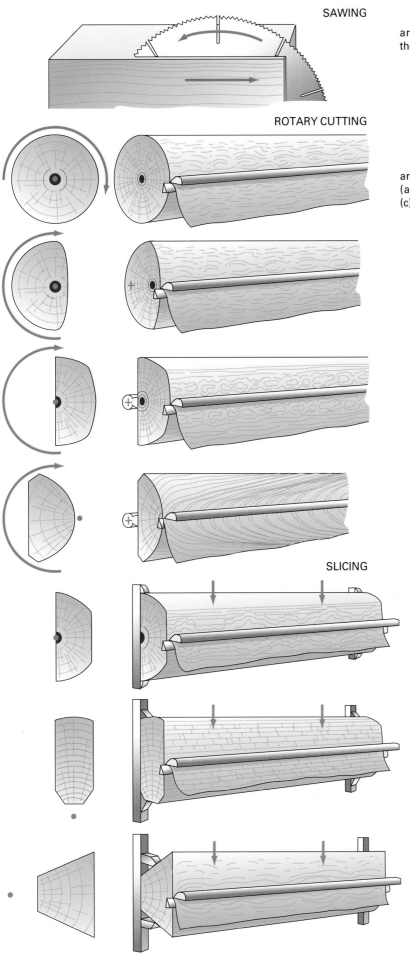

ROTARY CUTTING

SLICING

◄ Types of veneer that are obtained according to the cutting process.

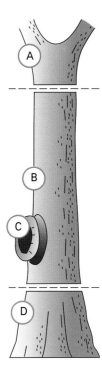

► Parts of the tree that are used for veneer: crotch (a), trunk (b), burl or burr (c), and butt or stump (d).

Adhesives

White Carpenter's Glue

This is water-soluble polyvinyl acetate (PVA). Its proper drying time is about 24 hours, although it can be speeded up by eliminating the water with the application of controlled heat. Once dry it becomes transparent, its residue is easy to remove, and it does not stain. It is the best choice for veneering jobs.

Rabbit Skin and Bone Glue

These glues are applied hot, and their preparation is labor intensive. They are obtained from boiling rabbit skins or bones and animal cartilage.

Quick Glue

This is also called contact cement. It has a bonding power that is almost instantaneous. It is not recommended because it does not allow for last-minute changes.

▼ White carpenter's glue (PVA) (a), bone glue in sheet form (b), contact cement (c), rabbit skin glue in granules (d).

Materials, Auxiliary Implements, and Tools

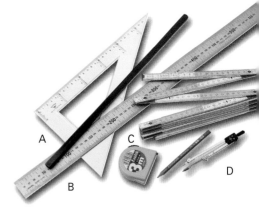

Double Boiler

A double boiler is used for preparing hot animal hide glue. After the glue has been steeped in water for some time, it is placed in a glue pot and heated; the glue is stirred constantly and water added as needed until the glue becomes liquid. The glue pot has a double wall, the outer part is filled with water. The water on the outside makes it possible to maintain a constant, mild temperature that prevents the glue from burning. This is why it is important for the water not to evaporate completely. Glue should never boil, or it would be ruined.

▲ Pot for glue and electric burner.

Adhesive Tapes

Adhesive tapes are used to hold together pieces of veneer, forming compositions that later will be glued, and to keep them in place while the glue dries, preventing the joints from shrinking and separating.

Masking Tape
This is the tape used by painters. It is thick and has a strong adhesive.
Gummed Tape
This is paper tape that has gum on one side. It must be wetted to stick.
Veneering Tape
This is an adhesive tape made of fine perforated paper 1 inch (25 mm) wide. It has a weak, water-based adhesive, making it easy to remove by wetting and scraping with a utility knife. Because it is so thin and it has small holes where the glue can pass through, it can be left under the sheet of wood when veneering.

Drawing Tools

Drawing tools are used for measuring, tracing, and cutting pieces of veneer. Rulers are used for measuring and marking the area of the wood surface that will be covered with veneer. The 30°–60° triangle is used to mark right angles. A long metal rule is the ideal tool for guiding the cut on the veneer.

◄ Orbital sander.

Sanders

Before a surface is veneered it must be thoroughly sanded. Any knot, alteration, unevenness, or irregularity could cause stability problems for the thin wood veneer—and it will be more noticeable once covered. An electric sander is the most practical, most efficient tool for sanding large areas thoroughly. Manual sanders are used for small areas.

Once the veneer has been applied and the glue is dry, any remnants of the bonding material (veneering tape) and irregularities are removed with a blade. Scraping should be done in the direction of the wood's grain, but if the grain varies across the various pieces, the blade should be passed across them diagonally.

Before applying the final treatment, the veneer should be sanded again, this time by hand if possible. This should be done by rubbing the surface with a sandpaper that is progressively finer and using sanding blocks to exert even pressure.

▼ Masking tape (a), gummed tape (b), water dispenser (c), veneering tape (d).

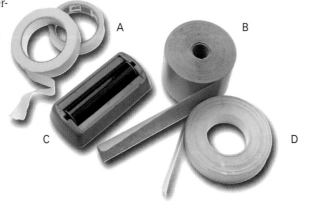

Utensils for Gluing

Different types of brushes are used to spread the glue evenly on the surface that is being veneered. Round brushes are the best for applying the adhesive to the corners and edges of the surface. A roller is useful for covering large surfaces, because it spreads the adhesive quickly and evenly. Paint scrapers can also be used to apply the adhesive.

Sheets of veneer are extremely thin, which makes them susceptible to humidity and to changes in temperature. When a veneer is placed on a surface covered with glue, it is actually being put in contact with a material that is largely made of water. This is why veneers on glue tend to swell and warp—and can cause great problems. To avoid them, the top side of the veneer is moistened with cotton strands or a cloth soaked with water.

▼ Toothed scraper (a), scraper (b), brushes (c), roller and tray (d), cotton strands (e), water (f).

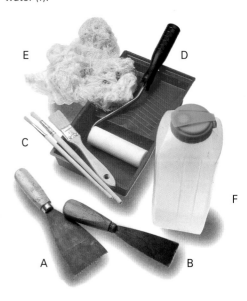

Finishes

The purpose of every finish is to protect the thin layer of wood and to highlight the basic qualities of the veneer: its color and grain.

A wood sealer seals the pores of the wood, leaving the surface smooth. Because it is toxic, a respirator should be worn when using it. Once dry, it can be polished with fine steel wool and sandpaper to prepare it for finishing with furniture wax or shellac. Wax is applied with a cotton cloth or strands, and when it is completely dry, it is rubbed briskly with a cotton cloth to make it glossy. The result is a satiny finish. The shellac highlights the grain and the design of the wood. It is applied in layers with a polishing pad.

▲ Wood fillers and respirator.

▼ Fine steel wool (number 0000) (a), fine sandpaper (number 400) (b).

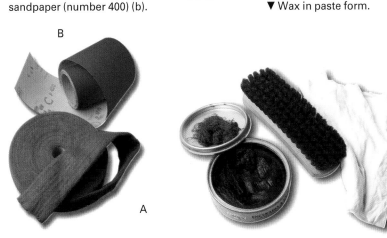

Tools for Preparation, Tracing, and Cutting

Toothed Plane
This is a plane with a toothed blade set vertically, used to prepare the surface for applying the veneer. The toothed blade makes small grooves in the wood into which the glue flows, producing an excellent bond.

Marking Gauge
This is used for scoring parallel lines on different sides of the wood to mark the needed dimensions. There is a type of gauge that is fitted with a blade that makes it possible to cut the veneer directly.

Veneer Saw
This has a blade with teeth on both edges. Cutting should be done from the outside in, perpendicular to the body of the operator.

Scissors and Utility Knife
These are used for cutting the veneer in curved sinuous shapes (scissors) and straight shapes (knife).

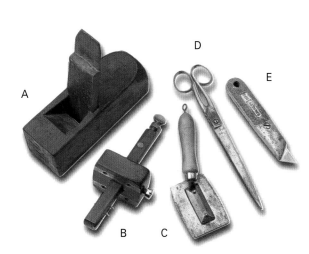

▲ Toothed plane (a), marking gauge (b), veneer saw (c), scissors (d), utility knife (e).

▼ Wax in paste form.

▲ Clamps for gluing in the shop.

Tools for Clamping and Pressing

Electric Iron
This can be any household iron. It is used to soften hide glue and to activate the drying process by evaporating the water from the white carpenter's glue or PVA.

Veneer Hammer
The shape of the veneer hammer is like that of a regular hammer, but the head is especially designed for pressing. It is used for applying veneer and for pressing and moving it in a zigzag motion to push excess glue and air bubbles toward the edges, to achieve a perfect bond between the veneer and the base.

Gluing Press
This can be made in the workshop; all that is needed are some clamps and some wood strips. The strips of wood must be larger than the piece that has to be glued, and the ends should be slightly curved. To press the glued ensemble, the strips of wood should be placed with the curved side facing down and clamped at each end, because there is the risk that by clamping the edges (the only possible place), the center of the wood will not receive enough pressure. In this case, the glue, instead of traveling to the sides, would remain in the center. By applying strips of wood that are slightly curved at the ends and clamping them, pressure is first applied in the center, and this forces the glue to spread to the sides.

▲ Electric iron and metal veneer hammer.

DECOUPAGE

This decorative technique involves applying paper designs by adhering them to the wood, in such a way that they appear to be part of the object. Decoupage is also known as "poor art," because it was used in the old days to imitate painted decoration. Although this technique was developed to substitute another that required much more skill and extensive experience, its continuous use and popularity have contributed to the creation of elaborate decorations of technical complexity. Furniture decorated with decoupage enjoys a widespread acceptance. Antique furniture decorated with "poor art" sells for high prices.

Basic Materials

Paper

Numerous types of paper can be used for decoupage. Prints or designs cut out from appliqué books or from magazines, small cards, doilies, and even photocopies are all possible sources. The only requirement is the weight of the paper, which must be heavy and durable so it does not wrinkle when it is glued to the wood.

◄ Prints, small cards, and doilies.

▲ Varnish (a), latex and water (b), brushes (c and d).

Adhesives

Different adhesives can be used to glue the paper to the wood.

Polyvinyl Acetate Glue (PVA)
This is also called white carpenter's glue. Water-soluble polyvinyl acetate is sold ready to use. Its drying time is 24 hours. It does not leave residue, and it becomes transparent when dry.

Gum Arabic
This is made from the excretions of different African *Acacia* species. It is water soluble. It is sold ready to use and is the most appropriate adhesive for gluing paper.

Glue Stick
This is a synthetic glue sold in stick form. It has little adhesive strength.

Instant Adhesive
These are glues made of different components, whose gluing power is almost instantaneous. They are not recommended because they do not allow last-minute changes.

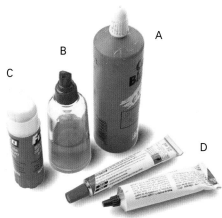

▲ PVA glue (a), gum arabic (b), glue stick (c), instant adhesives (d).

Protective Materials

Paper is by nature a fragile material that requires a protective coating. Varnish and latex are the ideal materials for this purpose.

Varnish
This is a synthetic protective material that is easy to apply with a brush or a spray gun. Varnishing with a spray gun is fast and produces a glossy, smooth surface. It is also used for creating brushstroke effects on the decoupage.

Latex
This is a water-soluble compound of synthetic resins. Several layers of this substance are applied to even out any small difference in height that exists between the paper and the wood, thus creating a thick layer.

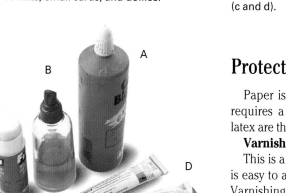

◄ Varnishing spray gun.

Finishes

The finishes for this technique do not differ from the ones used for wood. A wood filler is used for the first layer, which when dry is sanded using steel wool and sandpaper. Wax is applied to the second layer, which is polished with a cotton cloth. A respirator and neoprene gloves should be worn when applying the wood filler.

▲ Thin paper (a), tracing paper (b), markers (c), erasers (d), pencils (e).

Cutting Tools

Several cutting tools are needed to cut out the desired paper motifs. Sharp scissors make long cuts as well as rounded shapes. Utility knives with disposable blades are ideal for making straight and precise cuts. A craft knife with replaceable blades is used for small cuts that require precision.

Drawing Tools

When the arrangement of the paper designs is planned on the wood surface, a pencil drawing is made of the chosen arrangement using graphite paper and tracing paper, which will be used as the template.

Markers are also used, preferably dark colors, to conceal the borders of the paper by coloring them.

▶ Scissors (a), utility knives with disposable blades (b), craft knife with replaceable blades (c).

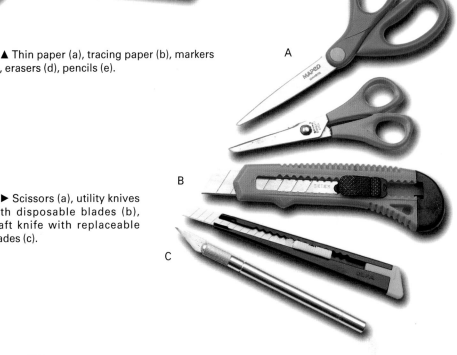

▼ Wax, cotton strands, and cloth.

▶ Wood filler (a), steel wool (b), sandpaper (c).

STAINING AND BLEACHING

*C*ertain decorative techniques have the peculiarity of having only the chromatic values of the wood in common. Wood changes or modifies its color completely without changing any other aspect whatsoever. The grain and figure are visible and other characteristics can also be appreciated such as its hardness, flexibility, porosity, and so on.

Processes that modify the color are staining and bleaching, as well as restoration of the color and protection of the wood. Staining involves the application of a liquid coloring dye that impregnates the wood, instead of being laid over it to form a surface coat. Bleaching gives the wood a tone lighter than the original one, through the application of bleaching products. To restore the color and protect the wood, products that are made for this purpose are applied, penetrating and impregnating the wood.

Basic Materials

▲ Natural coloring agents: walnut shell (a), tea (b), saffron (c), brazilwood *Caesalpinia bahamensis* (d), logwood *Haematoxylon campechianum* (e).

▼ Mordants: iron sulfate (a), potassium dichromate (b), tannic acid (c), copper sulfate (d).

Dyes, Colorants, and Mordants

Dyes are prepared by mixing the coloring materials with a solvent. Wood colorants can be natural or synthetic, according to their origin.

Natural Colorants

These can be derived from powdered vegetable substances—like logwood, walnut shell, and so on—or from certain animals or minerals. Those most commonly used colorants for staining wood are nogaline (walnut shell extract), tea, saffron, brazilwood, and logwood, among others.

Synthetic Colorants

These come from synthesizing chemical products. Anilines are usually used for dyeing.

The most common solvents for both types of colorants are water, alcohol, and mineral spirits or essence of turpentine.

The dye must meet certain requirements to be able to correctly stain the wood: penetrability (achieved with the appropriate solvent), stability, and transparency. Some dyes are made of coloring agents, which once applied to the wood, are not stable under light. Stability and color permanence are achieved with mordants.

Mordants

These are chemical compositions that are applied to wood that has been stained, as a fixative for the color. Products like vinegar, ammonia, and sulfuric acid are used as mordants. Other mordants—like iron sulfate, potassium dichromate, tannic acid, and copper sulfate—are dissolved in water. The latter can also be used by themselves as dyes. In the case of light-colored woods, the tannic acid is used to prepare the surface before the dye is applied.

Natural Dyes

Traditionally, wood staining was done with the same products that were used for dyeing fabric—that is, natural colorants. These dyes are obtained in extract form by boiling vegetables. However, because it is difficult to foresee their exact results, it is essential to carry out several trials before the final application.

Synthetic Dyes

These can be some of the chemicals used as mordants dissolved in water or a solution of anilines in water or alcohol. In the first case, the use of neoprene gloves, a mask, and eye protection is recommended.

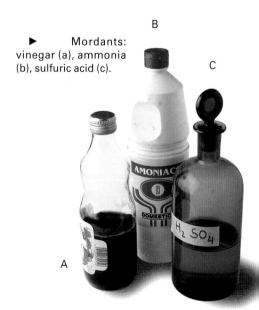

▶ Mordants: vinegar (a), ammonia (b), sulfuric acid (c).

◀ Aniline in bulk.

• Water-soluble aniline dyes: These are prepared by dissolving the aniline in hot water and shaking frequently. Although they are the easiest dyes to apply, unfortunately they raise the wood's grain. They are used for all types of projects, because they produce a uniform finish. The solutions can be stored for a long time, adding a few drops of bleach to prevent bacterial growth.

• Alcohol-soluble aniline dyes: These are anilines that are dissolved in alcohol. They come in a greater variety of colors than the water-soluble ones. Their problem is the alcohol evaporates quickly and the brush-strokes or application becomes visible. This makes it difficult to achieve even surfaces. Therefore, these dyes are only used for specific processes.

Different dyes applied on different woods produce different results. In the same way, the use of different mordants with various dyes produce different results.

▼ Water-soluble anilines.

▶ Alcohol-soluble anilines.

Bleaching Products

Products applied to wood to lighten its color.

Oxalic Acid
A supersaturated solution of this acid in water is prepared by mixing the oxalic crystals in hot water until there is a portion of the product at the bottom that has not dissolved. It is applied hot, and after it dries, the crystallized acid must be washed with plenty of tap water until it is completely eliminated. A respirator and eye protection must be used when handling it. Some products contain oxalic acid dissolved in water together with other additives.

Sodium Hypochlorite
This is common bleach. It is a powerful cleaning and bleaching agent and should be diluted before application.

Concentrated Hydrogen Peroxide
This is a widely used bleaching agent. It is a 30 percent concentration of hydrogen peroxide and should be neutralized with water after the desired tone has been obtained.

▲ Bleaching products: hydrogen peroxide (a), sodium hypoclorite (b), oxalic acid and water (c).

Products for Restoring Color

These are used to return the color to wood that is old or that has been repeatedly exposed to harsh weather conditions. These products are made with natural and artificial oils and wax that can be mixed with mineral spirits and essence of turpentine. The products impregnate and lubricate the wood, restoring it without creating a surface coat. Linseed oil is the product most widely used for restoration and serves as a base for different compounds.

Linseed Oil
Linseed oil is obtained from pressing crushed flaxseeds. The best quality oil is the one that results from pressing it cold. A variety with more impurities is obtained from hot pressing.

▶ Products for restoring color: linseed oil (a), vegetable oil compounds, resins and waxes (b), compound of linseed oil and essential oils (c). Solvent: essence of turpentine (d).

Protective Products

These are applied to protect the wood parts of exterior objects. They provide a natural finish. They are made from water-soluble synthetic resins, so they do not form a coating on the wood's surface.

Latex
This is a mixture of water-soluble synthetic resins that have a milky appearance. It dries fast and leaves a transparent finish on the wood.

UV Resistant Paint
This is a photoresistant product made from synthetic resins. It contains a product that filters ultraviolet (UV) rays.

▶ Protective products: latex (a), UV-resistant paint (b). Solvent: water (c).

Auxiliary Tools

Measures and Containers

Measuring devices are essential for calculating exact proportions when preparing dyes and bleaches. It is necessary to measure identical proportions or amounts of dye and solvent to consistently obtain a specific stain with the same color tone. A scale that can hold a container should be used to weigh solids. Laboratory graduated glass containers should be used to measure the volume of liquids.

It is a good idea to have different glass containers with lids on hand to store the solvents, as well as others for preparing and saving mixtures.

▼ Measures for liquids and containers for mixtures.

▼ Scale.

Implements for Heating

An electric hot plate with a temperature regulator should be used to heat and boil the materials in the processes that call for it. Certain vegetable-derived colorants must be boiled to prepare the extract that will be made into dye. The oxalic acid bleaching solution is prepared with the water that has been previously heated. Anilines are dissolved in hot water.

▲ Pot and electric hot plate.

Applicators

Flat brushes and cotton strands are most commonly used for small and medium surfaces, round bristle brushes for applications in corners and rounded areas. A roller and sponges are recommended for large surfaces, because they produce an even application and save considerable time and effort.

▶ Round and flat brushes and cotton strand

▶ Roller and tray and sponges.

Sanding and Polishing

After sanding the wood thoroughly, the surface is ready for the dye.

Water-based dyes open the pores of the wood and raise the grain; this is eliminated by scrubbing with a vegetable pad in the direction of the grain and then wiping with a cotton cloth.

▼ Vegetable scouring pad and cotton cloth.

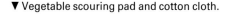

▼ Various pieces of sandpaper of different grit.

Finishes

Once the wood has been dyed or bleached, it is protected with the most appropriate finish for the job.

Wood Fillers

Nitrocellulose varnish is used for sealing the wood's pores. The resulting coat is not very hard; therefore, it scratches easily. It is preferably used as a preparation for subsequent wax finishes, because it gives the wax a satiny appearance (or a shiny one on shellac). After its application and once dry, any scratches are removed by polishing with a steel wool pad or fine sandpaper.

Wax

This substance gives the wood a satiny appearance. Wax is sold in liquid, solid, powder, or paste form. It is applied with cotton strands or a cloth. Once it is completely dry, it is polished briskly with a clean cotton cloth.

Shellac

This is an animal resin in flake form that can be purchased by weight and in various colors. Its preparation is fast and easy; the products needed are simply 7 ounces (200 g) of shellac and 1 quart (1 L) of alcohol. The mixture is poured into a bottle and shaken until the flakes have completely dissolved. Different concentrations can be prepared for different uses. It always contains a certain amount of impurities, which must be removed before it is applied. There are also various types of shellac available that are ready to use. The most common method of application is with cotton strands or a polishing pad. Only occasionally is it applied with a brush. The application of shellac with a polishing pad is difficult and labor intensive, and it requires a controlled environment. It provides a finish that equally highlights the beauty of the wood and its imperfections. Despite all that, it is a finish of great quality.

◄ Wood fillers and cotton strands.

▼ Petroleum jelly (a), alcohol (b), thick shellac (c), light shellac (d), polishing pad (e).

► Powdered wax (a), tinted wax (b), liquid wax (c), wax in paste form (d).

▼ Number 0000 steel wool pad and 360-grit sandpaper.

*T*his chapter covers the technical aspects of the decorative processes applied to wood following the order of the various techniques explained in this book: painting, gilding, pyrography, punching, inlay, marquetry, veneering, decoupage, staining, and bleaching.

The painting processes are explained first, including the differences between the water-based techniques and the oil-based techniques. This is followed by the gilding technique, where traditional and modern techniques are explained, as well as imitations in working with wood. Pyrography and punching are two techniques that require specific processes that do not vary in their application, and therefore they are covered in the same section. Although the techniques required for inlay and marquetry have some similarities, causing them to be confused with one another, it is safe to say that they are quite different; however, they are both covered in the same section and the differences and common traits explained. The inlay technique illustrates the required processes according to the material and the type of piece that one wishes to inlay in the solid wood. Marquetry processes are ordered according to the degree of difficulty of the job. The veneering section points out certain similarities shared with marquetry, although the procedures used for each are quite different.

Then, the traditional veneering method and the systems for creating different patterns are covered. Decoupage uses a specific and simple process in which successful decoration can be achieved with little skill. Finally, the last section covers the various staining processes, types of bleaching techniques, and the different protective procedures for the wood.

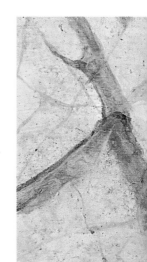

Technical
Aspects

Painting on any surface is an artistic expression as old as mankind. In fact, among the first discovered human activities are the decorative painting of living spaces (caves) and of artifacts and utensils. The first type of paint was, without a doubt, created from mineral and vegetable pigments and animal fat. Through history, wood has been a much-appreciated material. Proof of this is that until modern times furniture was passed down as heirlooms, specifically described in wills. However, most of the time, the characteristics of the wood (if it was not high quality) were covered with painted decoration. Painting was a fast procedure, it adapted well to the size of the carvings (if any existed), and its cost was proportionally less than any other type of decorative treatment. It also allowed making copies, in a more affordable version, of other expensive decorative processes: gilding, inlay of gems, and veneering with precious materials, among others. Wood is a porous material by nature, a characteristic that may cause adhesion problems for the paint. This inconvenience is solved by priming the wood before painting, with materials that seal the pores, making the paint easier to apply and more likely to adhere to the wood.

Water-based Techniques

Water-based paints are those that incorporate water in their formulas and have water as a solvent. The best known water-based product is tempera paint (see tempera technique). Others are beer-based paints and those that use latex and acrylic compounds. The last two are modern developments, resulting from the synthesis of plastic materials and synthetic resins.

Stamping and Stenciling

Stamping involves making an impression using a stamp charged with paint. The image is printed by pressing the stamp on the surface that one wishes to decorate. The stamps can be hollow or flat. The former makes an impression of just the outline, whereas the flat ones mark the whole surface.

Stenciling is based on the same principal but the procedure is slightly different. The shape that is transferred to the surface is cut out of a template. It is placed on the surface to be decorated, and the cut-out space is painted with light dabs, to prevent it from seeping under the stencil.

Without a doubt, stamping was one of the first painting techniques used in the history of mankind. The impressions of hands in the prehistoric caves are one of the first examples of painted decoration. Stamps have been used to decorate wood continuously through the history of art, but they have been restricted almost completely to the decoration of popular furniture, with a repertoire of motifs that is constantly repeated.

The modern technique of stenciling and its denomination derive from the technique that was used for printing the template or cartoon that would serve as a guide for the subsequent painting of a mural. The sketch was drawn on a piece of paper or cardboard, and then the lines were retraced with a sharp awl until the template was completed. Next, this was placed on the wall and dabbed with a finishing pad charged with coal dust, gypsum, or other powdered pigment, to transfer the design to the surface.

▲ The first step consists of choosing a motif that will be reproduced on the stencil. This will be in proportion to the surface, in this case a frame, in terms of size and shape. There are books with designs of borders and decorations that are useful in the selection of a specific shape or motif.

Stamping Small Details

◀ 1. To create small stamps that require certain precision, it is a good idea to use material that is easy to cut and work with and that is durable and flexible. Erasers, for example, are commonly used. The chosen shape can be traced directly onto the surface of the stamp (if it is the right size) or it can be copied (when it is necessary to change the scale). In this case, a leaf (a detail borrowed from a border) has been drawn freehand on the surface of the stamp with a pencil, and it has been retraced using a pen.

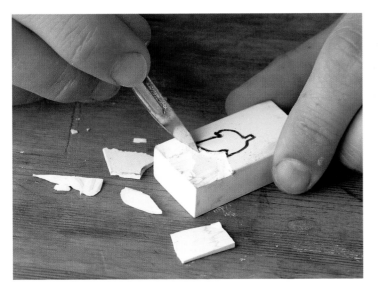

▲ **2.** The stamp will only reproduce the outline of the leaf; the inside will be hollow. The task begins by cutting out the outside area of the design with a scalpel. This tool has interchangeable blades of various shapes that can be used to make clean and precise cuts. Cuts should always begin on the outside edge of the outline and go outward.

▲ **3.** Next, the inside area of the leaf is removed. To do this, the scalpel is fitted with a small blade that has a sharp point, which allows precision work in tight areas.

▲ **4.** The outline of the motif in relief will stand out $3/32$ to $1/8$ inch (2 to 3 mm) above the surface of the eraser.

▲ **5.** Manipulating small stamps can be difficult. To make the job easier, the stamp can be attached to a larger base fitted with a handle. Then, the back of the eraser is bonded to a block of plywood $1/8$ inch (4 mm) thick with PVA glue.

▶ **6.** A handle or knob is also glued with PVA to the center of the outside surface of the plywood. It is essential to let the glue dry completely (at least 24 hours) before using the stamp.

◄ **7.** The process of preparing the wood surface begins by thoroughly sanding the entire frame by hand and smoothing out the edges with a sheet of number 4 sandpaper, until the surface is flat and smooth.

► **8.** Priming is done by applying a coat of acrylic sealant with a number 6 ox-hair brush. This dries in about 2 hours, which helps move the project along.

◄ ▼ **10.** Once the paint is dry, the distribution of the planned motifs should be arranged on the area to be decorated. To do this, the surface (the sides of the frame) and the shape of the stamp are measured to calculate approximately the number of impressions and their placement.

▲ **9.** The surface is covered with a commercial latex paint (for this project, mango color), applying it with a number 6 ox-hair brush, this being the most appropriate one, given the size of the area to cover.

◄ **11.** Using a number 2 brush, the navy blue latex paint is applied to the outline of the leaf. The amount of paint will depend on the intensity of the impression that is desired, so it is a good idea to make several tests before the final application.

► **12.** The impressions should be carefully made on the wood, with special attention given to their distribution.

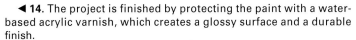
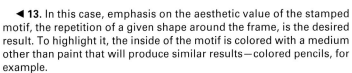

◄ **13.** In this case, emphasis on the aesthetic value of the stamped motif, the repetition of a given shape around the frame, is the desired result. To highlight it, the inside of the motif is colored with a medium other than paint that will produce similar results—colored pencils, for example.

◄ **14.** The project is finished by protecting the paint with a water-based acrylic varnish, which creates a glossy surface and a durable finish.

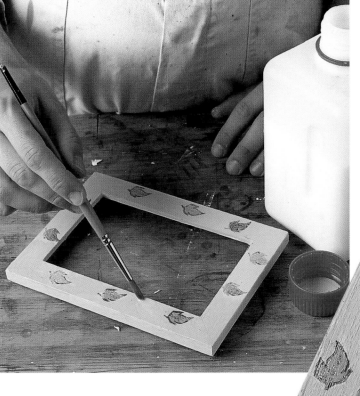

► **15.** The wood frame decorated with stamps has been given a new aesthetic value.

Stamping Medium and Large Motifs

◄ **1.** Another system for making impressions on wood involves making stamps where the surface of the motif is what is printed. In such a case, Styrofoam is one of many materials that can be used. The chosen motif is drawn or copied onto the Styrofoam sheet, and then it is placed on the cutting mat and cut out with a sharp blade. The mat has a soft surface that helps guide the cut.

◄ **2.** When the surface has been sanded, two layers of acrylic primer are applied to seal the pores of the wood. When the primer dries, a coat of paint is applied, which is prepared by mixing 2 parts white plastic paint with 1 part latex and universal tint. The latex will give the paint transparency and some glossiness. The tint provides the desired color; therefore, the more tint that is used, the more saturated the paint color will be.

◄ **3.** After making sure that the paint on the surface of the wood is dry, the stamp is covered with commercial plastic paint using a bristle brush. Next, the stamp is glued to a small plywood block and tested several times, also pressing the stamp onto paper, to eliminate any excess paint. This step should be carried out more or less often, depending on the intensity of the impression wanted.

▼ **5.** To finish it, the paint is protected with a layer of water-based acrylic varnish, which provides gloss and durability.

► **4.** After all the motifs have been printed with the stamps, the sides of the tray are painted with commercial plastic paint, which will be more opaque than the one used on the bottom of the tray.

Stenciling

◄ The stenciling template is attached to the wood, which should be well sanded, using masking tape. Sometimes the wood has some type of preparation and even background paint. The paint is applied using a bristle brush with a square tip, not overly charged, with small dabbing movements. This way, the paint does not smear and run under the template.

Using Beer-based Paint

Beer may be used as a binder to make paint that imitates the characteristic grain of the wood. The paint mixture contains beer with sienna pigments added. Because of the special characteristics of the binder, the technical process requires specific, unique steps. First, the beer is mixed with the pigment, which will have been previously wetted so that it dissolves completely in the beer. The resulting mixture is liquid so it does not adhere easily to any surface. The application of the paint is carried out by first wetting the brush (usually one that has a wide tip) in soap, and then in the mixture. The soap acts as an emulsifier of the paint, helping it adhere to the surface. When the paint is still wet, water and grainy effects, similar to wood, can be achieved.

This decorative procedure is totally irreversible once it has dried. This characteristic, together with the fact that it is easy to apply, make this the ideal treatment for decorating large wood surfaces. Its use was established at the end of the nineteenth century and beginning of the twentieth century to decorate doors and door frames made of low-quality wood, imitating the color and characteristics of the grain of hard woods.

▲ **1.** The preparation of the wood begins by sanding the surface by hand with a sheet of number 4 sandpaper, until it is smooth and clean.

▲ **2.** A coat of white, matte enamel paint is applied as a primer. This is done using a number 24 wide bristle brush, and then letting the surface dry completely. Enamel is an oil-based paint that provides a smooth, hard surface, which makes it an ideal foundation for graining.

▶ **3.** The pigment, previously dampened with a little bit of water, is mixed with the beer. The amount for each ingredient depends on the size of the surface to be decorated and the saturation of the desired color.

▲ **4.** It is essential to add an emulsifier, to ensure the mixture adheres well to the enamel. This is why the brush is soaked with a common soap, after having been wetted, before it is dipped in the paint.

▶ **5.** This procedure is repeated for each brushstroke, until a thin layer of paint has been applied to the surface of the object. However, the paint layer will never be even, because it will spread and form puddles.

▲ **6.** The surface is rubbed with cotton strands or a cloth in one direction, to begin the graining process. This procedure is used to eliminate the excess paint and to mark the direction of the grain.

▲ **7.** The wood grain is imitated by dragging the graining comb through the paint.

▲ **8.** The characteristic knots are produced by making circular motions with the opposite end of the graining comb.

▲ **9.** When the paint is dry, a matte varnish for wood is applied with a brush, to enhance the effect.

◀ **10.** The enamel shows through the grain, creating an effect similar to the grain patterns of the wood.

Distressing

The distressing technique (also known as *décapage*, a French word derived from the verb *décaper*, which means scaling, crusting, deoxidizing) involves applying one or several layers of paint to the wood, which are partially removed when they are still wet. By removing part of the material, a characteristic effect is achieved: The wood surface or the primer becomes visible under the paint.

This technique is relatively modern and its use for decorating wood is gaining popularity. In fact, this technique was developed during the second half of the twentieth century, and it is used to mimic the natural wear and tear of antique furniture. The decorative trend nowadays is to use objects treated with distressing for furnishing interiors, and it can be seen mainly on new furniture or structural elements (like beams, doors, and so on) to give them the natural look of the patina that appears from continual use. Distressed surfaces are commonly treated with a finish, to give them the look of an old surface, with worn-out paint.

Antique Distressing

▲ **1.** The molding is placed on top of two wood sticks that hold it up and make painting it easier. The surface of the molding is prepared by applying a generous amount of an acrylic sealant to form a thick layer, using a bristle brush. The layer of primer must be thick because it will have to come through the paint.

▲ **2.** A mixture is prepared of 1 part latex to 2 parts plastic paint. A universal tint (according to the color saturation wanted) and water are added. The amount of water is one-third of the total volume; this thins the mixture and makes it easier to apply. The latex makes it transparent.

◄ **3.** After stirring the mixture carefully, it is applied with a bristle brush.

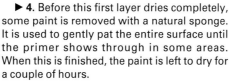

▶ **4.** Before this first layer dries completely, some paint is removed with a natural sponge. It is used to gently pat the entire surface until the primer shows through in some areas. When this is finished, the paint is left to dry for a couple of hours.

◄ **5.** For the second coat, a bright red universal tint is added to the previous mixture, and this changes it to a pinkish color. The paint is applied with the same bristle brush.

▶ **6.** Some paint is removed by gently dabbing the wet paint with a natural sponge, as was done with the first coat. By doing this, the yellow paint and the primer show through in certain areas. The paint is left to dry for 2 hours.

◄ **7.** The distressing is finished by briskly rubbing certain areas of the molding (the edges and places where a lot of paint has accumulated) with 360-grit sandpaper. By doing this, the surface is polished and the characteristic effect of a three-layer distressed surface is achieved.

▲ **8.** The antiquing process begins with the application of an oil-based shade. For this, blue, red oxide, and ochre paints are mixed on a palette, until the desired tone has been achieved. The mixture is applied to the molding with an ox-hair brush. Then, the entire surface is gently dabbed with cotton strands to blend the glazing and to almost entirely eliminate it from the high areas. When this task is finished, the oil paint is left to dry for 24 hours.

◄ **9.** To prepare the coat of varnish, a mixture is made of 1 part synthetic commercial varnish to 1 part linseed oil and a few drops of cobalt dryer. The linseed oil provides quality and transparency to the commercial varnish, and the dryer enables it to dry faster than usual. It is important to add the correct amount of dryer, or it could blacken the mixture.

► **10.** The varnish mixture is applied with a bristle brush and left to dry for 30 minutes.

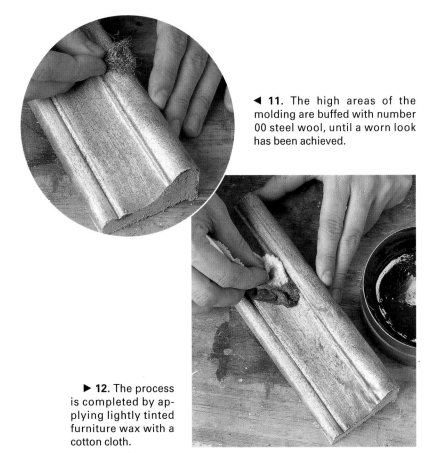

◄ **11.** The high areas of the molding are buffed with number 00 steel wool, until a worn look has been achieved.

▼ **13.** When the wax is dry, it is polished by buffing it briskly with a clean cotton cloth.

► **12.** The process is completed by applying lightly tinted furniture wax with a cotton cloth.

Using Tempera

With tempera, water is a medium that acts as a solvent for the binder as well as to dilute it. The main materials used in tempera are animal glues (such as fish and rabbit), vegetable glues (such as rye and starch), gum (such as arabic and tragacanth), dextrin, casein, wax, latex from figs, eggs, milk, and soap; all help form a suitable tempera to dissolve pigments and to form the paint. Tempera uses a water-based medium, but it is not soluble when it dries, and it can be repainted with more tempera or with oil-based products. Generally, when the colors are dry they are opaque, unlike oil-based paints, which offer the possibility of transparent treatments and glazing.

Casein is a protein substance that results when milk sours and the curd separates from the whey. It is not soluble in water; instead it forms a sediment to which an alkaline must be added to form a colloidal solution. Ammonia is usually used with paint, because it is volatile and leaves no residue. The result is a nonsoluble paint with flat, deep colors that become a little lighter when they dry. Since antiquity, casein has been used as an adhesive, and during the Middle Ages it was mixed with lime to glue together the wood pieces that were used to make altarpieces.

The tempera technique was already known in Byzantium (and probably in ancient Greece), from where it extended to all of Italy in the fourteenth century. In the Treatise of Theophilus (a priest from the eleventh or twelfth century), the method for preparing tempera, as well as casein-based tempera, is explained in detail. Initially, the term *tempera* included all paints that were made with techniques other than that of fresco; the term was later used to designate the paint made with egg yolk. Today, this name is given to any paint that is made from a water-based emulsion, which results in an opaque paint.

Casein-based Paint

◀ **1.** The preparation of the primer for the wood begins with the measuring of 5 ounces (150 g) of rabbit skin glue in granules.

▶ **2.** It is placed in a ceramic pot, and 1 quart (1 L) of tap water is added.

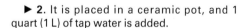

▶ **3.** The clay pot is inserted in a wider container of water and heated on an electric hot plate. This way the water with the glue is heated slowly and evenly, and the glue dissolves easily. It is important not to let the mixture in the clay pot boil, or it will be ruined.

▶ **4.** When the glue has dissolved completely and is still hot, whiting is added. The amount added will be equal to the volume of the glue mixture. It is stirred and put aside for 10 to 15 minutes, to give any air bubbles formed while stirring a chance to disappear, without letting the mixture cool completely.

◀ **5.** The first layer of tempera primer is applied with a bristle brush horizontally, with back and forth strokes.

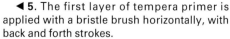

▶ **6.** Then, a second layer is applied in the opposite direction (vertical) and is left to dry completely. This technique, in addition to sealing the wood's pores, prevents any streaks that may form when the material accumulates on the surface.

◄ **7.** A spoonful of casein is placed in a bowl, preferably ceramic.

►**8.** Five spoonfuls of tap water are added and mixed with the casein.

▲ **9.** Next, two drops of ammonia are added with a dropper (a respirator should be worn). This product acts as an emulsifier and produces a colloidal solution.

◄ **10.** The mixture is stirred briskly until a paste with the consistency of yogurt is achieved. Wooden or glass utensils should always be used, because ammonia corrodes metal.

▼ **11.** A generous amount of powder pigment (in this case red) is placed in a different container, and tap water is added to cover it. The mixture is put aside. After 24 hours, the pigment is deposited on the bottom of the container, and the excess water must be removed, by tipping the container to one side.

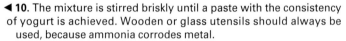

▼ **12.** The dampened pigment is mixed with the casein emulsion until a thick, homogenous paint is achieved. The previously dampened pigments dissolve completely and prevent the formation of lumps with the casein.

▼ **13.** The prepared paint is applied over the wood's primer with a sable brush.

◄ **14.** When the coat of vermilion paint that will be the background for the decoration dries, the surface is measured to arrange and center the chosen motif.

► **16.** A mixture of emerald green paint is now prepared following the previously described steps.

▼ **15.** The template and the graphite paper are attached to the surface with masking tape, and the decoration is copied onto the background paint. The carbon paper is yellow because this color will be easy to conceal when the motif is painted.

▲ **17.** The edges of the border are outlined and filled in using a number 4 sable brush.

▼ **18.** While the green paint is drying, the process is repeated to mix a yellow ochre paint. The details of the border are painted with yellow ochre, using a number 2 sable brush.

▼ **19.** The casein-based tempera colors are opaque, so the light colors, like yellow, can be applied over darker ones without a problem.

59

Oil-based Techniques

Oil-based techniques are mainly characterized by their use of linseed oil as a binding medium for the paint. Sometimes, varnish can also be used as a binder for pigments. In all cases, the solvent for oil products is either mineral spirits or essence of turpentine.

Oil paint is the most commonly used material for oil-based techniques. Vasari, in his treatise *Lives of the Artists*, dating back to 1550, attributes the invention of oil paint to Jan van Eyck, a fact that was refuted in the eighteenth century, whereby the invention was attributed to the author himself. It appears that the properties of linseed oil, walnut, opium plant, and hemp were known since ancient times, but their use in paints was limited to domestic or simple projects.

In fact, there is no evidence of their continuous use until the thirteenth century in England, where these oils were much used for decorative purposes. During the fifteenth century, improvements were made in the process of purifying linseed oil and some solvents. But it was during the sixteenth century that the materials and the techniques were developed enough to allow their use almost universally in the seventeenth century. Many opaque and transparent effects can be achieved with oil paints. The colors barely change when they dry, and handling and applying them is easy.

Combing

This technique involves forming lines or water effects in relief—that is, removing material by rubbing or scraping the surface of the still-soft layer of paint with a toothed rasp (called a comb) and exposing the lower layer. This is a mixed-media procedure, because a water-based technique is used for priming and for the first coat of paint; an oil technique is used for the rest of the top layers. Because oil paints dry slowly, paint may be removed and shapes created through which the base color shows through.

Historically, combing has been restricted mainly to simple furniture in the popular tradition.

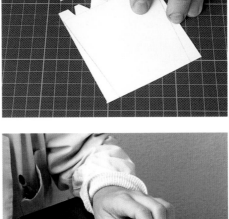

▲ **1.** A comb can be made by cutting a piece of cardboard into a 3¹⁄₄ × 3¹⁄₄ inch (8 × 8 cm) square with a craft knife on a gridded cutting mat.

◄ **2.** Teeth are drawn with a ruler on one of the edges. In this case the teeth are different in size and shape and are cut out with a knife. All the teeth are ³⁄₈ inch (1 cm) long.

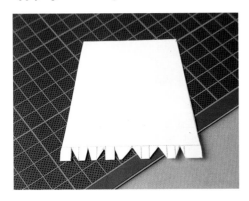

▲ **3.** The edge opposite the teeth serves as a handle. A ³⁄₈ inch (1 cm) diagonal cut is made along the sides to make it more comfortable to use.

▲ **4.** The knob is removed from the surface of the drawer to make the task easier.

◄ **5.** The base and the sides are protected with masking tape.

▲ **6.** The preparation of the surface begins by applying an acrylic sealer with a roller. This material, although diluted with water, is the most appropriate because it dries quickly (in about 2 hours). The wood on the front of the drawer was painted, and it is in good condition; therefore it does not require any further treatment.

▼ 7. Once the primer dries, a coat of paint is applied with a roller that will be the base coat of the composition. For this, the acrylic primer is mixed with universal tints (red and yellow), to make a salmon color.

▲ 8. In a solvent-resistant container, 1 part enamel and 1 part mineral spirits are mixed with the amount of oil paint necessary to obtain the desired color; the mixture is stirred with a wooden stick.

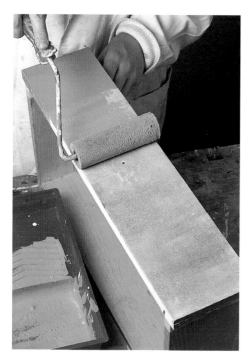

▶ 9. The mixed paint is applied with a bristle hair brush. Because the paint is quite diluted, it can be applied in thin layers.

▶ 10. Before the paint begins to dry, the comb is dragged with some pressure across the surface. This procedure drags and removes some of the top layer, leaving areas of the lower layer exposed.

▶ 11. The comb is carefully cleaned with clean cotton strands or a cloth. This way the comb can be reused without causing any stains. The layer of green paint is left to dry for at least 24 hours.

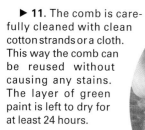

▲ 12. Another mixture similar to the previous one is made, but this time with yellow oil paint. This is then applied over the green color.

▶ 13. The combing procedure is repeated with the clean comb. When the paint dries, the protective tape is removed and the knob is replaced. It is not necessary to varnish the drawer front because enamel is a durable paint. The colors of the three layers are intermixed from being combed in opposite directions.

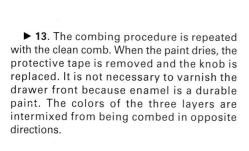

Marbling

This technique recreates or imitates marble through techniques used in painting. It is an oil technique and as such will require a water-based primer to prepare the wood.

Its use dates back to the period of the Roman civilization when murals decorated the walls of the chambers. It was also used, without a doubt, on furniture, imitating marble coverings or hard stone surfaces. The technique was used in medieval times to decorate the bases of altarpieces, certain liturgical objects, and wood furniture that in some cases perfectly imitated the surface of marble. During the Renaissance, and especially during the Baroque period, its use in the decoration of furniture and ornamental panels increased. Today, this technique is gaining popularity, especially in the decoration of furniture.

White-veined Marble

▲ **1.** Preparation of the wood begins with an application of acrylic sealer, using a roller, to minimize the pores of the wood.

▲ **2.** When it is dry, the entire surface is rubbed with a sheet of number 00 sandpaper to make it smooth and to eliminate any bubbles, which may occur from applying it with a roller.

▶ **3.** The first coat will be a white plastic paint applied with a wide brush. Painting should always be done in the same direction.

▲ **4.** A generous amount of a mixture in the proportion of 2 parts white plastic paint to 1 part latex is prepared in a tray. The latex will give volume to the resulting paint. The mixture is poured into three different containers.

▼ **5.** The paint in one container is mixed with a universal tint, creating a pastel blue color. When the plastic paint dries, this blue is applied with a spatula, making heavy applications in different directions. It is best to place the object that is to be painted on two strips of wood to make the job easier and to avoid staining the table.

▼ **6.** The procedure is repeated with two more colors, applying them in different directions and superimposing them. This way, a textured effect is created on the surface, also serving as the color on the final step. It is essential to let each color application dry for at least 4 to 5 hours.

▲ 7. A coat of white plastic paint is applied with a wide number 4 bristle brush and then left to dry for 4 to 5 hours.

▲ 8. The entire surface is sanded with 240-grit wet sandpaper. This will polish and smooth the surface, removing the brushstrokes and allowing the pastel colors of the background to come through.

▲ 9. To create the broken white tone of certain types of marbles, it is necessary to apply glaze over the acrylic paint. This is done by mixing oil paint (ochre and white in this case) with linseed oil and a couple of drops of cobalt dryer to make a paste of diluted and transparent consistency.

▲ 10. The glaze is applied using a bristle brush with a square tip.

▶ 11. Then, the surface is tapped softly with cotton strands or a cloth. This step should be done quickly, because the dryer speeds up the drying time of the paint. This way any brush strokes are eliminated and an even surface is created.

▲ 12. These steps are repeated with dark blue and ochre oil paints, to produce a color with some depth, similar to that of natural marble.

▲ 13. Other characteristics of marble are created by painting veins with oil paint that has been slightly thinned with mineral spirits and applied with a fine sable-hair brush. Veins are distributed over the entire surface and applied in different directions. The brush is twisted while it is dragged across the surface to make veins of different characteristics (like the natural ones). It is also helpful to use brushes of various thicknesses and different tones of paint, ranging from gray to black.

▼ 14. When this procedure is finished, the diffuser is used to gently brush across the surface following the direction of the veins, until they have been softened. It is a good idea to leave some areas untouched.

▼ 15. When the veins are dry (after 24 hours or so), a final varnish of oil paint in aerosol form is sprayed on—a fast and easy way to apply it. Application of liquid varnish always requires a higher degree of expertise, and there is a risk of removing part of the color of the veins if they are not completely dry. If liquid varnish is chosen, the piece should first be left to dry for several days.

Maroon Marble

▶ 1. The wood is prepared the same way as in the previous exercise. A coat of acrylic sealer is applied to the surface, and it is sanded after it dries. The painting process begins by mixing white plastic paint with black universal tint. The quantity depends on the area to be covered; however, the amount of tint used should always be minimal because of its strength.

▶ 2. The mixture is a light to medium gray and is applied using a bristle brush with a wide tip, always moving in the same direction. Because this coat is the background color and the base for the marbling, it is a good idea not to make it too dark.

◀ 3. In a container, 1 part matte synthetic varnish to ½ part linseed oil (in this case 2 spoonfuls to 1, respectively) are mixed. The mixture is then used as a medium to mix with the oil paint so that different strengths and gradations of color can be produced.

▶ 4. The bristle hair brush is dipped in the medium and mixed with red oxide oil paint on the palette. Painting is done on the dry background by drawing irregular shapes and later filling areas of the surfaces with different gradations of color.

▼ 6. The edges of the colors are blended by lightly tapping the paint with clean cotton strands or a cloth. The paint is then left to dry.

▼ 5. Ochre and white oil colors are added to the palette. Some areas are painted with these colors—following the red shapes, but not overpainting them—before the previously applied paint has dried. Interesting effects can be created by mixing colors in specific areas without blending the outlines.

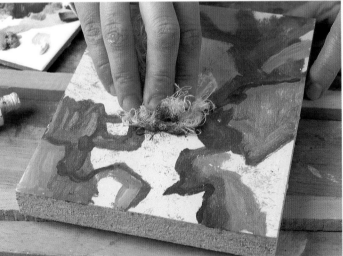

▼ **7.** Black and burnt sienna oil paints are added to the palette. Irregular water effects of uneven edges are painted with a medium sable-hair brush, following the edges of the existing colors. It is recommended that brushes of different thicknesses be used to get an interesting set of water effects: thin brushes for dark water effects and wider ones for light colors.

▲ **8.** While the paint is still wet, the surface is lightly tapped with cotton strands to give it texture.

▲ **9.** The white veins are painted with a thin, round sable brush (number 0). The irregular veins are made by twisting the brush cross-wise. They must always be painted with undiluted oil paint, diagonally or across the dominant design of the marble.

► **10.** To imitate the characteristic inclusions of the natural marble, raw umber oil paint is heavily diluted in the previous mixture of varnish and linseed oil and spattered on specific areas of the surface. A bristle brush with a square tip is generously wetted in the mixture and flicked from about 8 inches (20 cm), by pulling back the hair on the brush with one finger and letting it go.

▼ **11.** The paint is left to dry for about 24 hours. After this time, a spray varnish is applied as done before and for the same reasons.

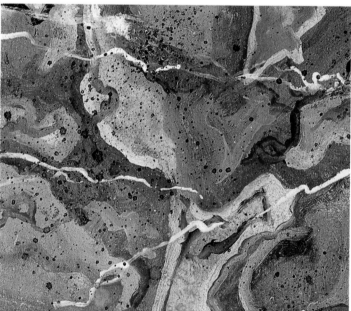

Patina

A patina is a thin, transparent coat that is applied over paint, gilding, or wood. It modifies the existing color, imitating the typical effects of the passage of time or wear and tear. The decorated base is always visible under the patina, which can be of one or several coats of paint and applied using different techniques.

The use of patinas in the decoration of wood is a modern phenomenon. Although at first they were mainly used to simulate an antique look, lately they have been used to achieve creative effects, colors, and textures, which are far from old or antique looking.

Here, four different techniques are applied directly over the primed wood, which best demonstrates the decorative result of each. There are, of course, many more techniques and decorative solutions, which could fill a book just by themselves; however, the chapters on "Staining and Bleaching" and "Gilding" offer even more about the antiquing techniques and the section on "Oil-based Techniques" even more about oil-based glazing.

Spattering

▼ **1.** The wood is primed to cover the pores by applying a coat of acrylic sealant. When it dries, the areas for each of the patina samples are separated with masking tape.

▼ **3.** The surface is painted applying continuous brushstrokes with an ox-hair brush. The result will be a transparent coat of uneven color, due to the natural properties of the shellac. Then it is left to dry for 30 minutes, until the shellac becomes tacky.

▼ **2.** Liquid shellac is mixed in a container with walnut-color alcohol-soluble aniline in powder form. Because the shellac is made with alcohol, the aniline should easily dissolve. A small spatula is recommended for adding aniline in minimal quantities, because it is a strong dye, and the tone of the mixture must be light.

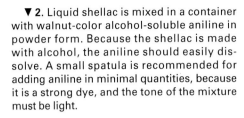

▼ **4.** A thick, round bristle hair brush is dipped in 96 percent alcohol. The painted surface is splattered from a short distance, bending the hair of the brush back with a finger of the hand that is not holding the brush and then letting it go. This will spatter the alcohol and partially dissolve the semidry shellac, creating blotches and drips.

▼ **5.** Spattered walnut-color shellac.

Rag Rolling

▲ **1.** A mixture of liquid shellac and a small amount of orange-color alcohol-soluble shellac is prepared as in the previous example.

▲ **2.** The primed wood surface is painted with an ox-hair brush, applying the mixture with large brushstrokes. Then, it is left to dry for about 1 hour.

▲ **3.** Shellac and black alcohol-soluble aniline are mixed in another container and applied over the orange coat. The alcohol in the black mixture should dissolve and cause some of the orange paint to streak.

▼ **4.** The second coat is left to dry for about 30 minutes. Still wet, it is rubbed briskly in different directions with a handful of clean cotton strands, removing material. The result is a brown surface (from the mixing of orange and black), which creates light and dark areas on the base color (in this case white).

▼ **5.** Ragged orange and black shellac.

Antiquing

◄ **1.** In a solvent-resistant container (preferably ceramic), asphalt is diluted with mineral spirits until the desired tone is achieved. Asphalt is a strong dye, so it is a good idea to use it in moderation and to dilute it generously.

▼ **2.** The surface is painted using an ox-hair brush. It is difficult to create an even surface with asphalt.

▶ **3.** The wet paint is dabbed with a crumpled cotton cloth. This produces a diffused and soft finish with three-dimensional effects.

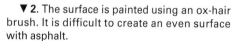

▶ **4.** The patted antique finish.

Color Glazing

▼ **1.** In a container, 2 parts linseed oil to 1 part mineral spirits and a couple of drops of cobalt dryer are combined. This mixture serves as the medium for diluting oil paints as well as for speeding up their drying time.

◄ **2.** A small amount of dark blue and lemon yellow oil paint are put on a palette, as is a container with the linseed-oil mixture (which in this case is in only one of the two containers). The bristle hair brush is dipped in the mixture and then on the palette with some of the blue paint, making a fluid, transparent glaze to be used for painting.

◄ **3.** Next, the entire surface is patted with cotton strands or a cloth to soften the brush marks. It is then left to dry for a couple of hours.

▼ **4.** The process is repeated using the lemon yellow oil paint, which is applied over the blue coat. The results are two strongly colored layers of glazing.

▼ **5.** Blue and yellow glaze.

Other Decorative Techniques

There are many decorative finishes that can be created with paint. From simple ones like rag rolling (which consists of dragging a rolled rag on the surface when the paint is still wet) and sponging to more complicated ones like marbling and trompe l'oeil, the combinations are endless. Below are small samples of each.

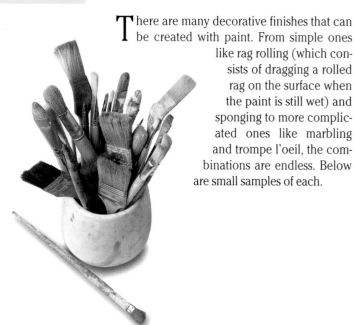

▲ Rag rolling.

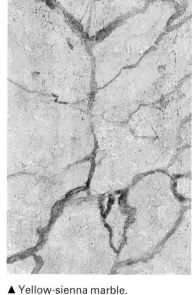

▲ Yellow-sienna marble.

▲ Aquamarine marble.

▲ Malachite.

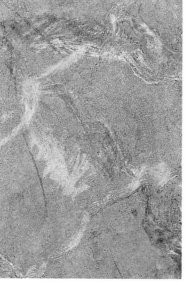

▲ Green-veined marble.

▲ Combing.

◄ Red granite.

◄ Lapis lazuli.

▲ Mottled gilding.

▲ Antique gilding.

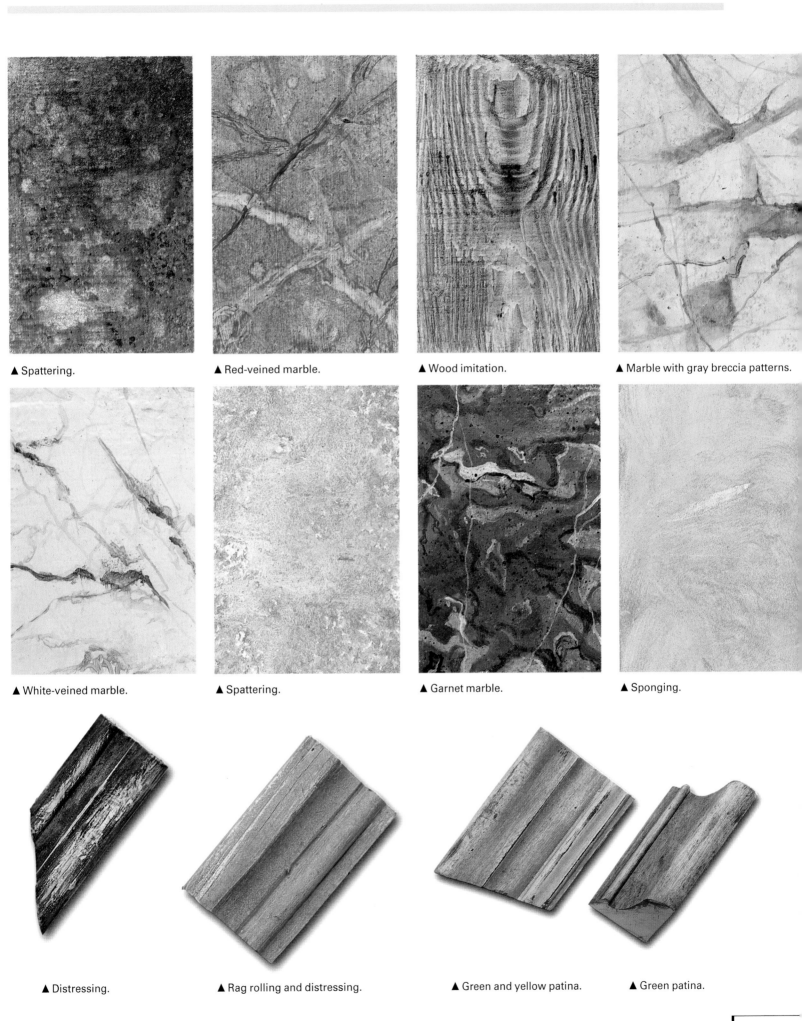

▲ Spattering.

▲ Red-veined marble.

▲ Wood imitation.

▲ Marble with gray breccia patterns.

▲ White-veined marble.

▲ Spattering.

▲ Garnet marble.

▲ Sponging.

▲ Distressing.

▲ Rag rolling and distressing.

▲ Green and yellow patina.

▲ Green patina.

GILDING

*G*ilding *is the technique of attaching sheets of gold leaf to a surface that can be wood or any other material. The term* gilding *is used to refer to the use of metal leaf of any kind. The techniques used for working with gold have been practiced since antiquity. The remains of old civilizations provide information related to the methods of metal extraction, fusion, and elaboration. We know that the gold was pounded repeatedly with a hammer, beating it until thin sheets were produced. The gilding was done by interposing a preparation of various inert materials between the surface and the metal leaf so it would not break during application. The gilding technique has been used to decorate wood throughout the history of art, from ancient Egypt to present times. During the medieval period, it was used on most pieces of religious furniture (to a lesser degree on nonreligious furniture) and on altarpieces, to decorate architectural elements and backgrounds as well as to imitate clothing and drapery when combined with painting techniques. Gilding was also popular during the Baroque period. Together with painting, it became the main decorative technique used on the elaborate altarpieces, interiors, furniture, and architecture.*

The Gilding Technique

The traditional gilding technique is known as water gilding. Because it involves applying the gold leaf using water as the adhesive, it is a water-based technique. This process requires elaborate priming of the surface and the use of materials that require much preparation, such as rabbit skin glue and the clay base called bole. Although it is possible to burnish the gold to an intense gloss when it has been applied using this technique, today that is only done in high-quality projects and in the restoration of works of art.

The gilding technique that uses an oil base is called mixtion gilding. It appears that gilding was sometimes done using oil methods in the past, but its use has become more popular lately because the preparation is commercially available. Its use requires less skill than water gilding because the base does not have to be prepared as carefully and the drying time is longer, which makes it easier to apply.

Today, size is used in water gilding, rather than the slow, involved traditional techniques. Size is a water-based varnish that is ready to use when purchased and is a replacement for the traditional adhesive. It should also be mentioned that bole is not commonly used (in fact, it is only used for the traditional water gilding), and it has been replaced by commercial paints of similar colors. The availability of new materials, like leaves made of various metals and different alloys of the traditional metals, allows for the exploration of new decorative avenues in water gilding.

Relievo can be considered a combination of media and is the result of mixing two different techniques: gilding and painting. It involves making drawings on the gilded and painted surface by scraping, until the metal leaf is exposed.

The Gilder's Pad

This is the tool that the gilder uses for holding and cutting the gold leaf. It is essential for working efficiently because it provides a flat, soft, and rough surface, which holds and keeps the gold leaf in place, free from oil that would cause it to become adhered.

Making a gilder's pad that perfectly fits the personal needs of the user is a simple task.

◀ 1. A piece of wood 6 × 4 inches (15 × 10 cm) long and ³/₈ inch (1 cm) thick is purchased or cut in the shop. Then, a piece of felt ¹/₄ inch (3 cm) larger on each side than the wood is marked with a pencil and cut.

◀ 2. The felt is stapled to the sides of the wood. First, the center of each side is stapled, pulling the fabric taut. Then, stapling continues toward the corners, along the opposite sides. The fabric is tucked under at each corner.

▲ **3.** A piece of chamois identical in size to the felt is cut and stapled in the same way. A diagonal cut is made in each corner, which makes it possible to overlap the two edges of the chamois to form a perfect angle.

▲ **4.** Then, the surface of the chamois is sanded with number 6 sandpaper to remove the nap. This produces a rough, even surface that is helpful for handling the gold leaf.

▲ **5.** To make the handle and the gilder's knife holder, a strip of chamois about 6 inches (15 cm) long and ³/₄ inch (2 cm) wide is needed. The edge of this strip is stapled to the middle of the upper part of the back side of the pad. A thumb is placed under the chamois so that the strip wraps around it and can be stapled to the wood. The handle is completed. Then the procedure is repeated with the handle of the gilder's knife so a practical surface is created. Finally, the excess strip is cut off.

▲ **6.** To prevent small drafts from carrying off the gold leaf, a protective shield is made with parchment paper. This type of paper is rigid enough to provide protection, is easy to cut and fold, and requires minimum storage space for the cushion. A 14 × 5 inch (35 × 12 cm) rectangle is marked and cut.

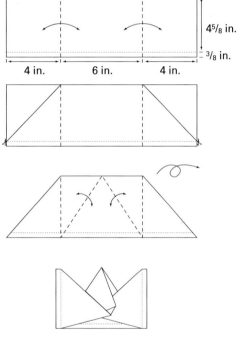

▲ **7.** The paper is folded and cut following these steps.

▲ **8.** Next, the paper is stapled to the sides of the pad at the edge that meets the handle on the back.

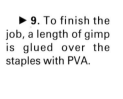

▶ **9.** To finish the job, a length of gimp is glued over the staples with PVA.

▶ **10.** Then, thumbtacks are used every 1¹/₂ inches (4 cm) to reinforce the attachment of the various materials to the wood base, giving it a finished look.

▼ **11.** The gilder's pad is ready to be used.

Water Gilding

Water gilding involves covering a surface with gold or silver leaf using the following technique. The wood is prepared with a primer made of rabbit skin glue and whiting, which, when dry and sanded, is covered with several coats of bole. Then, the leaf is applied using a solution of water and rabbit skin glue as adhesive. The finish can be matte (if the bole is left as is) or glossy (if it is burnished with an agate stone).

A similar technique was probably used in ancient times for covering objects with gold. The careful examination of objects from ancient Egypt that have survived to present times provides valuable information about the gilding technique. In those days, gold was beaten until fine leaves were obtained; then the leaves were applied over the prepared base—a neutral material that was polished, homogenous, and durable. The technique—altered slightly due to the mechanization of the gold leaf's manufacturing process and the discovery of new materials—has been preserved to present times.

▲ **1.** The process begins with the preparation of primer for the wood surface. First, 5 ounces (150 g) of rabbit skin glue in granules is weighed.

▲ **2.** Then, 1 quart (1 L) of tap water is added and put aside for 24 hours so the glue softens as it soaks. It is a good idea to store this mixture in the refrigerator because the wet glue tends to rot and lose its adhesive properties if exposed to high temperatures.

◄ **3.** The mixture is heated gradually in a double boiler until the glue becomes completely liquid and smooth. It is important to never boil the glue, because it would lose its adhesive properties.

◄ **4.** While the mixture is still hot, a coat of glue is applied to the wood surface with a wide brush; it is then left to dry. This first layer seals the pores of the wood, making it less absorbent.

When the glue gets cold, it acquires a jelly-like consistency. If this does not happen, it may be that the glue has spoiled or that the proportions and measurements are not correct.

▼ **6.** A layer is applied in one direction with a wide brush, and it is left to dry completely. Then, the concentration of whiting is increased gradually so the preparation does not develop a crust, and it is applied in successive layers (up to four) in opposite directions (horizontally to vertically). For the last layers, the concentration of whiting is reduced to make a soft, flexible surface that will allow the gold leaf to be polished.

◄ **5.** Then, 6 spoonfuls of whiting are added to the hot glue and the mixture is heated, without letting it boil, until it dissolves completely and becomes a clear liquid.

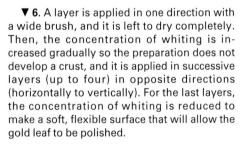

▲ **7.** The primer is briskly sanded in a vertical direction, using number 00 sandpaper.

▲ **8.** Next, the surface is sanded horizontally with 360-grit sandpaper to make it completely smooth.

▶ **9.** Following the steps as explained before, 2¹/₂ ounces (70 g) of rabbit skin glue granules are weighed and diluted in 10 ounces (300 ml) of tap water.

▲ **10.** An amount of 1³/₄ ounces (50 g) of liquid glue is weighed and put aside.

◀ **11.** An additional 1³/₄ ounces (50 g) of liquid glue is weighed and heated in a double boiler. An equal amount by volume of commercial bole is added. The mixture is stirred until it is smooth.

◄ **12.** The surface is painted with vertical brushstrokes, while the mixture is still hot. It is left to dry.

► **13.** The second coat is applied horizontally until the layer is even. It is left to dry completely.

◄ **14.** A sheet of gold leaf is placed on the gilder's pad and cut in the desired shape, depending on the base or area to cover. Then it is put aside.

► **15.** The glue that was previously put aside is heated and applied over the layer of bole. Only an area the size of the cut gold leaf is covered.

◄ **16.** The gilder's tip should be dampened with petroleum jelly to pick up the gold leaf from the gilder's pad. To do this, a small amount of the liquid is placed on the back of the hand.

► **17.** The gilder's tip is rubbed across petroleum jelly to wet its bristles.

► **18.** The gold leaf is picked up holding the gilder's pad with one hand and the gilder's tip with the other. The petroleum jelly acts as a mild adhesive allowing the fragile material to be handled.

◄ **19.** The gold leaf is applied over the area that has been covered with liquid glue.

▶ **20.** The gold leaf is gently tapped with the gilder's mop to adhere it.

▶ **21.** The wood base is covered using the following technique: The gold leaf is cut, the glue applied, and the leaf set. Special care should be exercised when placing the leaves. The edges should overlap slightly to ensure a continuous surface.

▶ **22.** When the covering procedure is finished, the surface is brushed with the gilder's mop to remove any excess of gold leaf.

▲ **23.** The rabbit skin glue is left to dry for 24 hours. Afterward, the gold is burnished by rubbing the surface gently, always in the same direction, with an agate burnisher.

▶ **24.** The fragile leaf of gold is protected with a layer of shellac, which is applied with a badger hair brush.

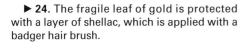

Mixtion Silver Leaf Gilding

The technique of gilding (used in the wider sense of covering a surface with metal leaf) with mixtion is much easier than the traditional water technique. The mixtion is an oil-based varnish that is sold ready to use, and it is simple to apply. It has a slow drying time, between 12 and 15 hours, so larger areas may be worked than with water gilding. It is ideal for gilding when it is mordant (tacky) (see the section on materials). Mixtion gilding gives the covered surface a characteristic matte look, because it does not allow the metal leaf to be polished.

Although mixtion is considered a recent technique, it is believed that in ancient times oil media were used as a base for certain types of gilding that were not polished.

In the following example, mixtion gilding is explained using a simple substitute for the bole, made with a mixture of shellac and powder pigments.

Antique Gilding

▼ **1.** The project begins with the preparation of the primer for the wood. To do this, 9 ounces (265 ml) of shellac flakes are weighed and put in a glass jar with a tightly fitting lid. (Shellac always requires the use of a glass container.)

▼ **2.** Next, 1 quart (1 L) of 96 percent alcohol is added, and the jar is closed to prevent evaporation. The jar is shaken periodically, until the flakes are completely dissolved. It is not necessary to filter the mixture because the shellac will not be used for finishing.

▲ **3.** The molding is placed on top of two wood sticks that serve as supports, making the work and the handling of the wood easier. A coat of shellac is applied with a brush to seal the pores of the wood to make it less absorbent. Shellac dries fast because the alcohol evaporates quickly.

▲ **4.** To make the bole substitute, about 5 ounces (150 ml) of shellac are mixed with some red ochre pigment in powder form until a fluid and homogenous paste results. The amount of shellac used depends on the size of the surface to be gilded. The proportion of the pigment is greater or lesser, depending on the tone desired for background.

◀ **5.** A coat of shellac tinted to imitate the bole is applied with an ox-hair brush.

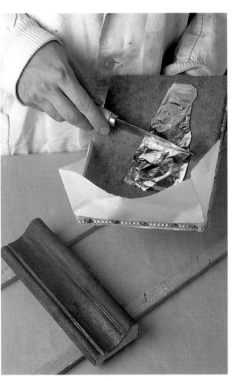

▲ 6. Without waiting too long, because the mixture of pigment and shellac dries quickly, a coat of the mixtion is applied over the entire surface. The product is applied straight from the container with a soft brush.

▲ 7. The surface is rubbed with a fingertip to make sure that it is not sticky. Next, a silver leaf is placed on the gilder's pad and cut to the desired shape with the gilder's knife.

▲ 8. The leaf is picked up with the gilder's tip, which was previously dampened with petroleum jelly (see the water gilding technique), and is carefully placed on the surface.

▲ 9. The silver leaf is arranged by tapping gently with the gilder's mop.

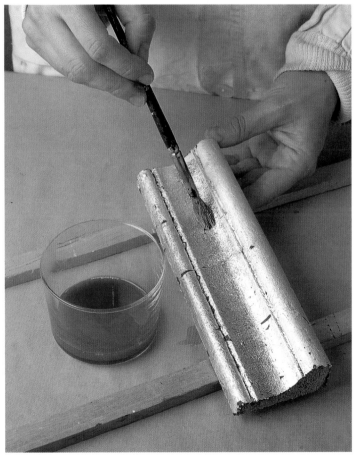

▶ 10. The process is repeated until the molding is completely covered with the silver leaf. Then the molding is put aside so that the mixtion can dry completely (the amount of time needed is usually indicated on the container). Next, a coat of shellac (without the pigment) is applied to protect the silver leaf.

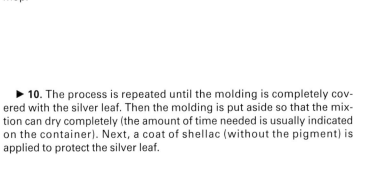

▲ **11.** Then, asphalt is applied to darken the silver and produce a finish that resembles natural aging. This substance has great covering and dyeing capabilities, so thinning it is always recommended. To do this, 1 part of asphalt is diluted in 3 parts mineral spirits.

▲ **12.** The surface of the molding is painted with the thinned asphalt using an ox-hair brush.

▲ **13.** Talcum powder is applied to give the low areas the characteristic dusty look of old molding. Small amounts are spread around with a natural-bristle brush.

▲ **14.** Material is removed from some parts of the molding to complete the antiquing process. The high areas are sanded with number 00 steel wool, partially removing the asphalt or the silver leaf.

◀ **15.** The result is a new molding that is a perfect imitation of an old one.

Relievo

This technique involves covering the gilded layer completely with paint. Once dry, the paint is removed by scratching certain areas to make decorative motifs or designs. This way, the gold shows through the lines of the drawing, producing a rich effect. In general, mixtion or size is used to gild the surface; relievo does not require burnished gold leaf because it is only visible in small areas.

When this technique originated, it was used for painting in medieval altarpieces, to imitate quilted material, rich clothing, and damascene pieces that the nobility used. This technique produced realistic effects, simulating the quality of material made from velvet and gold thread.

The project illustrated below explains the relievo technique with tempera paint, following traditional procedures. The gold leaf is applied over a mordant size, using acrylic paint as a substitute for bole.

▲ **1.** The primer is prepared by weighing 2¹/₂ ounces (70 g) of rabbit skin glue granules.

▶ **2.** Next, 1 quart (1 L) of tap water is added and it is left for 24 hours to allow the glue to soften (see the water-gilding technique).

▶ **3.** The mixture is heated in a double boiler, without letting it boil, until the granules dissolve. A coat of hot glue is applied to the wood using a wide brush and then left to dry. This layer seals the pores of the wood, making them less absorbent.

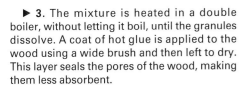

▲ **4.** The color of the bole is imitated by applying a layer of red acrylic paint, using a bristle brush.

◀ **5.** When the acrylic paint is dry, a small area of the surface that is to be gilded is painted with the commercial size.

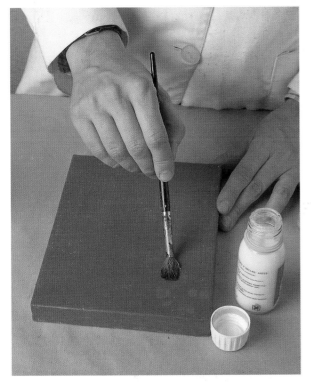

◀ **6.** A gold leaf is placed on the gilder's pad and cut to the required size with a gilder's knife.

◄ **7.** The gold leaf is picked up with the gilder's tip, which has been dampened with petroleum jelly (see the water-gilding technique).

◄ **8.** The gold leaf is placed over the sized area.

◄ **9.** Next, the leaf is adjusted and tapped gently into place with the ox-hair mop.

► **10.** The process is repeated until the entire surface is covered (see the water-gilding technique). When the size is dry, the excess fragments are brushed from the surface with the ox-hair mop.

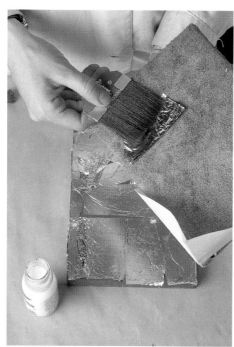

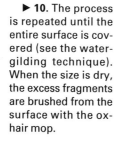

▲ **11.** The tempera technique produces a matte paint with great covering power that is easy to work by scraping when it is dry. Gum arabic in powder form is needed to prepare the tempera, so the granules are placed inside a clean cloth and pounded with a hammer.

► **12.** The yolk of an egg and a heaping teaspoonful of powdered gum arabic are mixed in a container, preferably glass.

► **13.** Water is added to the mixture, using the egg shell as a measure. One of the shell's halves is filled with water twice and added to the mixture twice, and then it is stirred with a plastic or wooden spoon.

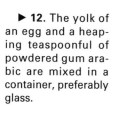

▼ **14.** The powder pigment (in this case sienna color) is dissolved in tap water until it becomes a creamy paste. Next, it is added to the tempera mixture to color it. It is recommended that the colored tempera be warmed slowly in a double boiler so all the ingredients bind completely. Excessive heat will cause the egg yolk to curdle.

► **15.** The warm tempera is applied to the gold leaf using a badger-hair brush, without painting over any brushstrokes.

▲ **16.** When the tempera paint is dry, the chosen design is traced over it. White graphite paper (which will stand out against the dark paint) is placed directly on the base under the tracing of the design. The papers are held in place with tape to prevent them from moving.

▲ **17.** The drawing is traced with a sharp pencil. When the procedure is finished, a perfect copy should appear on the painted surface.

► **19.** To finish it, an varnish aerosol is applied; the aerosol makes the job easy and fast.

▲ **18.** The drawing is retraced with a wooden stick to remove the paint. Wood removes the paint without scratching the gold. Shading effects are produced by making fine lines with wooden sticks of various sizes.

PYROGRAPHY AND PUNCHING

Pyrography and punching are two different techniques, which nevertheless share common traits. They are both irreversible—that is, once they are applied it is impossible to return the wood to its original form. This is why it is always necessary to design and plan even the smallest detail of the decoration before starting the project. Unlike other decorative techniques, they also have in common that neither one adds any additional elements to the wood. They change its look without changing its nature: color, grain, figure, hardness, and so on. The history of these techniques has developed in parallel, even being used for the same purpose at certain times.

Pyrography

Pyrography involves darkening the surface of the wood with controlled heat. Different color gradations can be achieved through surface burning, creating a highly decorative look.

The process consists of tracing the motif or the chosen design (either copied or created) directly onto the wood. This is done by applying pressure with a pencil until a slight indentation is produced on the wood. Graphite paper is not used because it leaves a residue under the pyrography that is impossible to remove. Before starting the project, several tests should be done to check the intensity of the heat and the use and handling of the various tips. Next, the lines that serve as guides are traced with the electric heating iron, set at the desired temperature, and shading is added as necessary. The interchangeable tips make shading easier and are helpful for creating custom borders. When the process is finished, the traces of soot should be removed with a clean brush and any mistakes or excessive burning corrected by sanding the surface of the wood with fine-grit sandpaper.

Traditionally, pyrography has been used mainly as an auxiliary technique to one of greater importance, marquetry. The technique makes possible the application of intricate shading or details on the veneer. It was also used in popular furniture as a substitute for painted decoration. It was widely used in Italy during the fifteenth and sixteenth centuries to produce decoration on furniture with a refined tradition, almost becoming a fad. It was used on large trunks depicting mythological and courtship scenes and on small trunks decorated with scenes of courtly love. In both cases, the background was worked using the punching technique, which accentuated the relief in the scenes.

▼ **1.** The first step, before starting with pyrography, is to choose the design or decorative motif that will be printed on the wood. Because elaborate designs require some skill, beginning with geometric motifs or simple designs is recommended.

▶ **2.** Next, the most appropriate tool and tips are chosen, based on the selected design. Performing several tests on scraps of wood to get comfortable with the burning iron (if it burns the wood a lot or a little) and the use of the tips is recommended before starting the project.

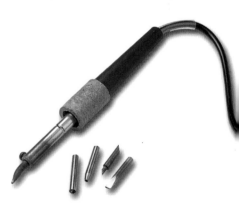

▶ **3.** The first task is to sand the wood thoroughly with 150-grit sandpaper. This makes the surface flat, even, and smooth, which is essential for good results. Pyrography involves burning the surface of the wood, so if it is not in perfect condition, the results of the burning (even when the heat is applied evenly) will not be consistent.

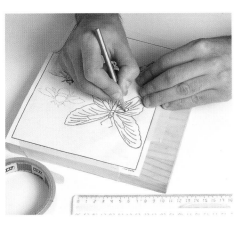

▲ **4.** The lines that will serve as guides for the design are traced on the wood, using a ruler and pencil. A drawing of a butterfly has been chosen in this case, so a center line is also drawn. Next, the chosen design is copied directly onto the wood by attaching the sheet of paper to the base with masking tape. The wood is marked by tracing the outlines of the butterfly with a pencil, which results in a slight indentation that serves as the basis for the project.

▲ **5.** When the temperature of the burning iron has been regulated, the design is slowly traced with it. In this case, a fine point is used because the design has a linear motif.

▲ **6.** Many motifs can be used as borders by using points of different shapes. Here circular and oval points are used to make two different samples of borders.

▶ **7.** When the pyrography is finished, the guidelines are removed with an eraser. Next, traces of ash are removed with a soft brush, and any areas that were too burned are evened out by sanding them with 180-grit sandpaper.

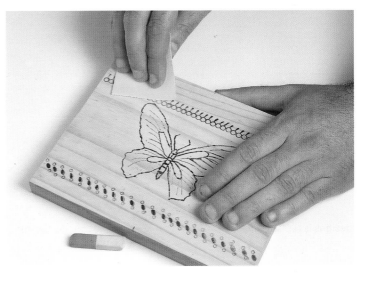

▲ **8.** Decorations done with pyrography are durable, so a protective finish does not need to be applied, except in those cases where the specific use calls for it. Here, a lightly tinted furniture wax has been chosen, and it is applied with a cloth or cotton strands.

▶ **9.** When the wax is dry, the surface is polished with a clean cotton cloth. Pyrography is a simple way to make permanent decoration on wood.

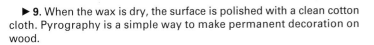

Punching

Punching consists of marking wood by striking it to make a relief effect in the background of a design or shape. The punches used for this project have a design carved into one end. As in pyrography, and for the same reasons, the design is made directly on the wood. It is done by placing the punch vertically on the wood and striking the end with a hammer with a nylon head. It is struck once for each mark, always with the same pressure to create similar marks. This is especially important if the punching is used to decorate a background; therefore, the wood must not be wavy or uneven.

Punching has always been used as an auxiliary technique to embellish the backgrounds of big and small chests decorated with pyrography (as mentioned before) or to decorate more or less visible areas of furniture. It was used in Catalonia during the fifteenth and sixteenth centuries to decorate the borders of gothic chests.

▲ 1. The design should be drawn before punching begins. Here, the object to be decorated (a folding music stand) is made of several assembled pieces, forming a regular structure with spaces in between. First, the outline of the wood is traced to get a life-size drawing.

▲ 2. Next, based on the available punches, a sketch is made with the chosen design, drawing it freehand on paper with a pencil.

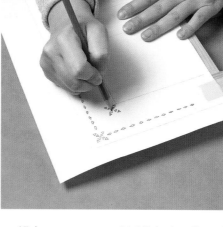

► 3. The entire surface of the wood is sanded thoroughly with 150-grit sandpaper. Next, the design is transferred directly to the wood, attaching the paper in place on the music stand with masking tape and tracing the design by applying some pressure to the pencil. The result is a lightly marked drawing that will serve as a guide for the project.

▼ 4. The punch is placed on each mark in a vertical position, and the end is struck gently using a hammer with a nylon head. It is important to only strike once on each mark and with the same force so that the indentations made are identical.

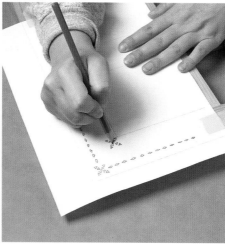

◄ 5. In some cases, to highlight the effect of the punching, for example on a border, it is a good idea to add color to the wood. Here it is lightly stained with undiluted asphalt, applied with cotton strands.

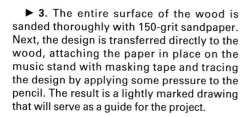

▼ 6. Next, the color of the asphalt is blended while still wet, by wiping it with a clean cotton cloth. The punched marks with the original color stand out against the wood stained in a dark color.

▼ 7. The surface of the wood is protected with a coat of nitrocellulose varnish because the decorated piece is used on a daily basis. The varnish is applied with clean cotton strands, using neoprene gloves and a respirator for protection. The piece is then left to dry.

INLAY AND MARQUETRY

Traditionally, inlay and marquetry have evolved together and, on many occasions, they have even been confused. They have often been considered as two different aspects or variations of the same technique, although in reality they have so many differences that they must be treated as different techniques. However, they belong to the same family of decorative techniques. The confusion between them has continued throughout the history of art. Both techniques have almost always been combined in the same decoration, which has perpetuated the confusion.

Inlay

Inlay involves decorating solid wood by inserting pieces of different materials into incisions and cutouts made for that purpose.

The first traces of this technique appeared in some friezes made of stone during the Protodynastic period, in Egypt. This civilization left many examples of furniture decorated with gem inlays, semiprecious stones, pieces of precious metals, and exotic woods. During the Roman period, rooms and furniture were decorated with marble and semiprecious stones. After the Middle Ages, and because of

the Arab influence in the Iberian Peninsula, designs made with small triangles, diamond shapes, and strips called *mudejar* intarsia, became widespread. In Italy, *Carthusian* intarsia was developed, which is simply several strips or panels of marquetry formed by many minuscule pieces, which are sometimes inlaid in solid wood. For this reason it can be considered a specific type of marquetry. Inlay, as a technique, continued during more modern times (seventeenth and eighteenth centuries) with the use of exotic

woods and materials, such as mother of pearl and some metal alloys. Its use has continued to present times, but it has been limited to expensive pieces of furniture.

Inlaying a Marquetry Medallion

In the following illustration, a purchased marquetry medallion is inlaid into a chipboard with veneer on both sides.

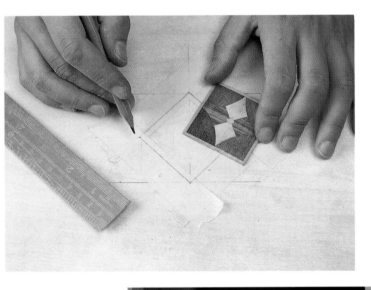

◄ **1.** First, the medallion is centered by measuring the board and marking the outline for the marquetry. Next, the area where the cut will be made is covered with masking tape to prevent the veneer from splintering. Then the outline of the piece is marked on the masking tape with a pencil.

▲ **2.** The piece of veneered chipboard is secured to the table with a clamp. The veneer is cut with a sharp knife, using a metal ruler as a guide.

◄ **3.** The veneer is removed with a chisel, being careful not to go beyond the mark of the outline of the medallion and not to remove too much of the chipboard.

▲ 4. Once the veneer has been completely removed, the glue that bonded the piece to the plywood is also removed by scraping with the chisel. This step must be done with precision, or any traces of old glue could cause adhesion problems with the new glue that will be used later.

▲ 5. After the pencil lines are erased, rabbit skin glue is applied to the chipboard with a wide brush, and the marquetry medallion is placed with the side that has the paper facing up. If the paper side is glued, the piece may come off sooner or later.

◄ 6. The board, protected with newspaper on both sides, is placed between two larger boards and pressed with two clamps (see the chapter on "Materials and Tools"). It is put aside for 24 hours so that the glue dries completely.

▼ 7. After this time, the press is taken apart and the paper protecting the marquetry removed. It is dampened lightly using only a wet cloth, because too much water would soften the glue and the piece would come off. The paper is completely removed by scraping it with the blunt edge of a spatula.

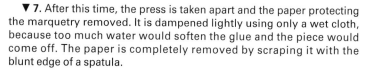

▲ **8.** When the surface is dry, it is sanded by hand with 150-grit sandpaper that has been wrapped around a block of wood.

▲ **9.** A coat of nitrocellulose varnish is applied with cotton strands to finish. Neoprene gloves and a respirator are used for protection.

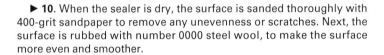

► **10.** When the sealer is dry, the surface is sanded thoroughly with 400-grit sandpaper to remove any unevenness or scratches. Next, the surface is rubbed with number 0000 steel wool, to make the surface more even and smoother.

▲ **11.** The process is finished by applying wax with cotton strands and polishing the dry surface with a clean cotton cloth.

► **12.** The result is a finely decorated panel.

Inlaying of Strips

The technique used to inlay strips varies according to the materials involved. The preparation of the wood, on the other hand, is always the same and involves marking it and removing material. The material the strip is made of determines the adhesive, the setting, and the finish. In this case, the inlay of a purchased strip of wood and another made of metal into hardwood is illustrated.

◄ **1.** The wood is marked with a double pin marking gauge. The area where the inlay is to be set with respect to the edge of the board and the width of the strip are marked. The marks left by this tool also serve as guides for removing the material later. Both points are adjusted by sliding the block that serves as the guide and one of the points.

2. The material can be removed by using two different tools to achieve the same results:

◄ The piece of wood is securely attached to the work table with two clamps. Next, the area between the marks is lowered by removing material with a $1/6$ inch (4 mm) mortise, by tapping its end with a mallet. It is also possible to use a cutting gauge or a marking gauge to carry out this task.

► The piece of wood is firmly set against a stop (this can be another piece of wood placed perpendicularly) and it is placed in line with the body. The manual router plane fitted with the small $1/6$ inch (4 mm) blade is pulled firmly between the marks left by the gauge, to quickly remove material from the area designated for the strip.

How to Inlay a Wood Strip

▲ **1.** White carpenter's glue (PVA) is the adhesive used to inlay a wood strip, because it works best for this material.

◄ **2.** The strip is then placed into the groove and is tapped softly with a hammer until its surface is flush with the wood. Then, any excess glue is removed with a cotton cloth or strands.

How to Inlay a Metal Strip

► **1.** Cold fish bone glue, which is sold in liquid form, is used to bond metal inlay strips. The glue is applied with a brush, and the strip is set in the groove.

► **2.** The surface of the strip is tapped with a hammer until it is set in place. The glue is then left to dry for at least 8 hours.

◄ **3.** The strip is worked with a metal file in a diagonal direction, until any protruding part of the strip is level with the wood.

► **4.** Finally, it is sanded thoroughly, using a special sandpaper for metals wrapped around a block of wood, to remove any marks that the file left.

How to Inlay Pieces of Wood

In this case, a design formed by pieces of sycamore and walnut are inlaid into a solid piece of African cedar. When inlaying wood, it is important to remove the material evenly and to make it deep enough so the pieces can be securely set in place. Here, because the area reserved for the inlay is quite large, a manual router plane is used for that purpose. A chisel is best if the area to be cut away is small.

◄ **1.** First, the motif is designed and a pattern made by tracing it out of a piece of cardboard. Then the exact location of the decoration is measured and marked (in this case this is done by drawing the center lines). The pattern is set on the mark (centered on the two lines) and the outline traced, marking the wood with a pencil.

◄ **2.** The piece of solid wood is secured to the work table with two clamps. The inside of the design (the area that is to be removed) is outlined by making cuts with the chisel, tapping its end with a wooden mallet. The chisel is used for hollowing the area, removing a first layer of wood about 1/12 inch (2 mm).

► **3.** Next, the manual router plane with a 1/6 inch (4 mm) blade is used to make a deeper cut, leveling the base of the wood.

▲ 4. This process has cut out an area of about 1/8 inch (3 mm), sufficient depth to inlay pieces 1/6 inch (4 mm) thick.

▲ 5. As a result of cutting and removing the wood, it is almost certain that the measurements of the design have changed slightly with respect to the original. To make sure that the pieces of inlay fit the real dimensions, it is essential to make a copy. A sheet of tracing paper is fixed to the wood with masking tape, and the design is copied by rubbing its edges with a pencil. The inside corners of the star are extended to mark the outline of each piece of the motif.

▲ 6. The sections that form the star have different dimensions. This is why each section is cut on the inside of the pattern to make sure that pieces match *before the wood is marked.*

► 7. The shapes are marked on the surface of the wood using the two cutout sections as guides.

◄ 8. The pieces for the inlay are cut from two different types of wood to make a color pattern. To do this, the bird's mouth jig (see chapter on "Materials and Tools") is attached to the table with a clamp, and the piece of wood placed on top is cut with the fret saw. It is important to cut on the outside of the pencil line, being careful not to remove it completely. When the process is finished, the pieces are inserted into the cutout area, and each space and its pieces are numbered.

◄ 9. The pieces may be of slightly different sizes. If this is the case, it may be necessary to sand their edges briskly on sandpaper, to make sure that they fit snugly against each other and that their seams are almost unnoticeable.

► 10. Carpenter's glue (PVA) is applied directly from the bottle, and each piece is set in its place.

◄ **11.** The piece of wood with the inlay is placed between two boards, inserting several pieces of newspaper (in this case) or wax paper to prevent the decoration from sticking to the board.

► **12.** The piece is pressed by firmly attaching a clamp to the middle of the board that is over the inlaid design. The pieces fit perfectly, so the glue is left to dry for 2 hours, which is sufficient time to make sure that the pieces are securely bonded. If they are out of alignment at all, pressure should be maintained for 24 hours, until the glue has dried completely. Then, the press is removed.

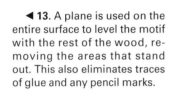

◄ **13.** A plane is used on the entire surface to level the motif with the rest of the wood, removing the areas that stand out. This also eliminates traces of glue and any pencil marks.

► **14.** The surface is sanded briskly with 150-grit sandpaper, to make it perfectly smooth and polished.

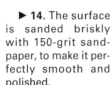

▲ **15.** The wood is soaked with linseed oil to deeply penetrate the wood without leaving any residue on the surface and to provide a protective coating.

► **16.** The completed inlay project.

Marquetry

Marquetry is the technique, although some consider it an art, of creating designs or geometric forms by inlaying small pieces of wood veneer (such as ebony or mahogany), pieces of metal (such as gold or silver), shells, or ivory in a wood surface, creating a level and continuous surface on the wood. It is a long, labor-intensive process, because the materials used are extremely fragile. Before cutting wood veneer, it must be reinforced by gluing paper to it. Also, small packets are made so that the veneer does not splinter or break and so that several identical pieces can be cut at one time. These tasks influence the working process, which requires making packets, taking them apart, and later pressing them to strengthen them. As can be seen, the technique is completely different from inlay and the process much more involved.

Decorating with marquetry dates back to ancient civilizations of Asia Minor and Egypt, where they used thin sheets of marble as decorative murals. The same technique was also used for wood furniture. The art spread widely during the Roman period, and it became more refined.

Wood marquetry work is also called intarsia. *Carthusian* intarsia is considered to be the first marquetry technique used during the medieval period. It owes its name to the Carthusian brothers (the order of Saint Bruno), who made small compositions from different woods, bone, ivory, and mother of pearl, forming geometric decorative motifs. This type of marquetry was done mainly during the fourteenth and fifteenth centuries in the regions of northern Italy.

A different type of marquetry, pictoric intarsia, depicted naturalistic scenes in perspective, like still lifes, geometric designs, landscapes, and tromp l'oeil. It is believed that they were first made in Sienna in the fourteenth century. The technique was heavily used in Italy during the fifteenth and sixteenth centuries to decorate furniture, entire rooms, and large surfaces, like choir stalls.

In Holland and Germany, marquetry acquired importance during the sixteenth and seventeenth centuries, where a kind of furniture was made that worked well with this type of decoration. Such furniture had big doors and panels that could be covered with various subjects. The colonization of overseas territories by Europe during the sixteenth and seventeenth centuries introduced the use of exotic wood to marquetry. In France, during the seventeenth century, the influence of the *Manufacture Royale des Meubles de la Couronne* caused marquetry to be considered of prime importance in Europe. André-Charles Boulle developed the technique using fine and expensive materials like mother of pearl, tortoise shell, copper, and gilt bronze.

During the eighteenth century, the use of marquetry became widespread in Europe, and local woods were combined with exotic species, such as palisander, rosewood, mahogany, and myrtle. Marquetry was also used as decoration in the nineteenth century, and it reached its peak during the Modern period, at which time it was often combined with other techniques and used on furniture, forming part of the overall concept of decoration. It is worth mentioning that Catalonia was one of the big centers of marquetry production during this period.

Marquetry with Commercial Inlay Strips

In this case, a deteriorated wood frame is covered with simple marquetry, carried out by combining sapele veneer and a strip of commercial inlay.

▲ 1. The length and width of the sides of the frame are measured. Next, using a sharp knife, the veneer and the strip are cut a little larger than those measurements so that there is enough material. The sapele is placed on a wood base.

▲ 2. The cut pieces are placed on a strip of masking tape, to make the desired shapes. In this case, the strip is inserted between two pieces of veneer of similar grain.

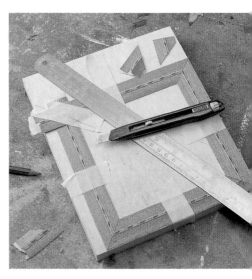

▲ 3. After this process is repeated for all the sides of the frame, the composition is arranged on a wood base by attaching it with masking tape. The dimensions are checked to ensure that they correspond to those of the frame. Then the angles are cut at a 45-degree angle. To do this, one side is placed over the other and cut at the desired angle with a knife, using a metal ruler as a guide.

▲ 4. The marquetry is bonded to the surface with contact cement made with cyanoacrylate. It is tapped lightly with the hammer to make sure that it adheres.

▲ 5. Next, the masking tape is removed, because the contact glue dries almost immediately.

◀ 6. The frame is turned over, leaving the side with the marquetry facing down. The excess veneer is cut off while holding it firmly in place. The cut is always made from the outside toward the center, to avoid splintering at the edge.

▼ 7. Next, the sides are veneered to make the surface of the frame consistent. Contact cement is applied to the pieces.

▼ 8. The veneer is attached to the sides by tapping them lightly with a hammer until the bond is made.

◄ **9.** The excess veneer is removed just like before, always cutting from the outside to the center to avoid breakage and splinters.

▲ **10.** The entire surface of the frame is sanded with 150-grit sandpaper wrapped around a wooden block. This step smoothes the wood and its round edges.

◄ **11.** A coat of wood filler varnish is applied with cotton strands, and then it is left to dry. Neoprene gloves and a respirator should be used for protection.

▲ **12.** To remove any traces of varnish, the surface is sanded with 400-grit sandpaper and then with a number 0000 steel wool pad.

◄ **13.** The result is an attractive marquetry frame, made following a simple procedure.

Geometric Marquetry

Anyone wishing to produce marquetry designs should begin with simple motifs with straight lines that are easy to cut. Geometric designs are appropriate for this. In the following example, a geometric design is made using myrtle wood, sapele, and walnut to decorate a sheet of medium-density fiberboard (MDF).

▶ **1.** The design is drawn with pencil and paper, according to the dimensions of the board. Next, the veneer is selected according to the color of the wood, the direction of the grain, and the design.

▲ **2.** To cut the veneer, it is placed over the design pattern and the sides marked, extending the lines at the corners. A metal ruler is used as a guide. The veneer has been cut in such a way that the grain of the wood will always be parallel to the hypotenuse (inner or outer side, according to the piece) of the triangle.

▲ **3.** The veneer is placed on a wood base and cut using a knife and a metal ruler.

▲ **4.** The veneer is arranged on top of the pattern and attached to the paper with a drop of white carpenter's glue (PVA).

▶ **5.** Any excess veneer is removed, and the motif is squared using a knife and a metal ruler as a guide.

▶ **6.** The procedure is repeated, and the veneer pieces that frame the composition are attached to the paper. After all this is done, the motif should be attached to the paper on the back side with the good side facing up.

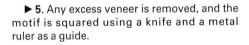

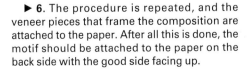

◀ ▶ **7.** However, marquetry should never be glued to the surface with the paper, because it may come loose sooner or later. To reinforce the pieces and bond them together, wrapping paper is attached to the marquetry surface with hot rabbit skin glue. The proportions for the adhesive are 2 parts rabbit skin glue in granules filled until covered with tap water and another part water to dissolve it in a double boiler.

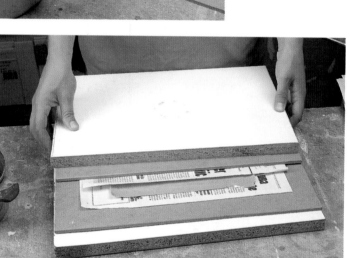

▲ **8.** Next, the marquetry with the attached wrapping paper is placed between two sheets of newspaper (to prevent it from sticking) under two masonite boards and between boards of solid wood slightly larger in size than the project.

▼ **9.** It is pressed with clamps (see the chapter "Materials and Tools") placed symmetrically to apply even pressure to the entire surface. The glue is left to dry for half an hour.

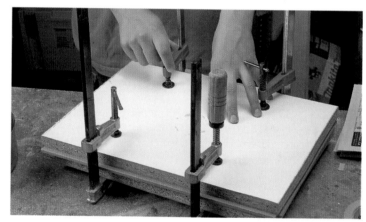

▼ **10.** The press is taken apart and the white paper with the drawing of the design removed. To do this, the surface of the paper is lightly dampened with a cloth soaked in tap water until it becomes soft. Then it is scraped with a blunt spatula until the layer of paper is completely removed, and the marquetry is left to dry.

▼ **11.** Finally, the marquetry is placed on the final MDF support. First, a layer of PVA glue is applied to the MDF with a wide brush.

▲ **12.** The marquetry is placed on the MDF with the side that has the packing paper on top. The sides are firmly secured with masking tape to prevent any movement while it is being pressed.

▶ **14.** Finally, the packing paper is removed. First, the surface is dampened with a cloth, then the paper is removed with a blunt spatula.

▲ **13.** In the same way as before, the marquetry on the MDF is pressed between two boards faced with Formica. (Formica is a nonporous plastic material that will not adhere to the marquetry.) The press is left for 24 hours until the glue has completely dried.

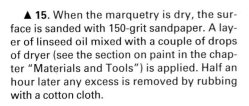

▲ **15.** When the marquetry is dry, the surface is sanded with 150-grit sandpaper. A layer of linseed oil mixed with a couple of drops of dryer (see the section on paint in the chapter "Materials and Tools") is applied. Half an hour later any excess is removed by rubbing with a cotton cloth.

▶ **16.** The MDF decorated with custom design marquetry.

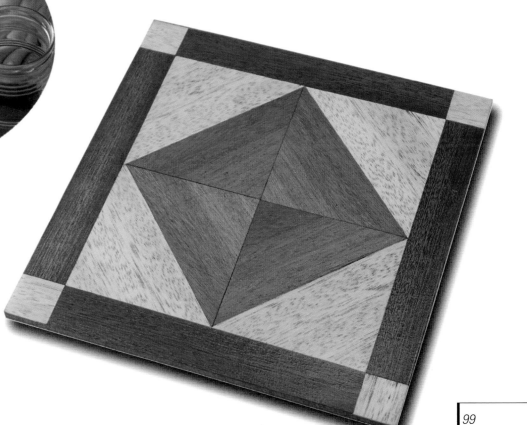

Creative Marquetry

This project is much more elaborate than the previous one. The design, copied from a pattern book, represents the outline of a salamander. The technique produces two versions (positive and negative) of the same design—and the most appropriate one can be chosen—because both the background and the shape are cut at the same time. The decoration, made of beech and sapele woods, is applied to a plywood board.

◄ **1.** Once the motif is chosen and photocopied, it is attached to the veneer with hot rabbit skin glue (see the technique on geometric marquetry). This way the veneer is protected by making it more rigid.

▼ **2.** The pattern is placed centered on the veneer, and it is protected with a sheet of newspaper to prevent it from adhering to the boards of the press.

▲ **3.** The pattern is pressed with the veneer; they are placed with newspaper between two masonite boards under two solid wood boards, which are held together with sticks and clamps, and are then left to dry for 1 hour.

◄ **4.** This process is repeated by attaching the top sides of four sheets of veneer to newspaper. The pieces of veneer include the one with the design to be cut out, a similar one in case the first one breaks, the one that will be the background of the composition and, finally, another one, which will be discarded.

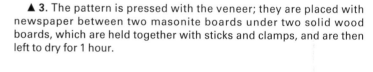

► **5.** A rigid packet should be made in order to cut the veneer properly. To do this, the pieces should be put together following the order indicated before, and nailing them together on a cork base using 1/8 inch (3 mm) long nails with flat heads.

▶ **6.** The packet of veneer sheets is separated from the cork, and the part of the nails that protrudes is cut off with pliers.

▶ **7.** The nails are tapped with a hammer, to prevent them from sticking out.

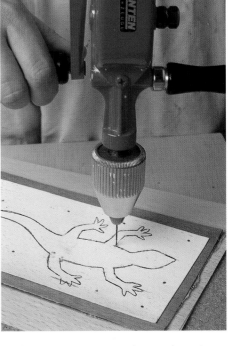

▲ **8.** To make the sawing task easier, a small hole is made with the hand drill in an area that is not visible or that is easy to conceal (in this case a corner) to insert the blade of the fret saw. The hole is made with the hand drill fitted with a $3/64$ inch (1 mm) bit and held vertically.

◀ **9.** The veneer package is placed over the bird's mouth jig, held in place to the work table with a clamp. The blade of the saw is inserted in the hole and the outline of the design cut.

▶ **10.** Five veneer cutouts are made of the salamander: the original design (a), the motif chosen for the marquetry piece (b), a similar piece in case the first one has to be replaced (c), another one cut from the wood veneer that will be the background of the composition (d), and the last one from a veneer that will be discarded (e).

▼ **11.** The package is taken apart by pulling out the nails with pincers. Once the top and bottom pieces have been discarded, the positive-negative combination that is considered the best is chosen.

◄ **12.** The two pieces of the composition are attached by gluing wrapping paper with hot rabbit skin glue (see the geometric marquetry technique) over the surface with the newspaper.

◄ **13.** The marquetry with the wrapping paper attached is placed between two sheets of newspaper, and the press is assembled as described before.

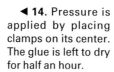

◄ **14.** Pressure is applied by placing clamps on its center. The glue is left to dry for half an hour.

◄ **15.** When the marquetry is taken off the press, hot rabbit skin glue is applied with a wide brush and the marquetry attached to the permanent base.

▶ **16.** It is placed in the press (protecting it with the same materials as indicated before) using wood pieces with clamps. The pressure is maintained for 24 hours until the glue has completely dried.

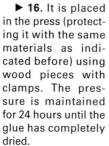

▼ **17.** When the time has passed, the double layer of paper is removed. First, it is rubbed with a handful of cotton strands soaked with tap water to dampen and soften it.

▲ **18.** Next, it is scraped with a blunt spatula until it comes off. The marquetry is left to dry.

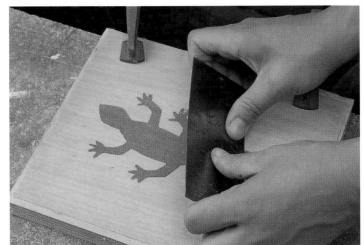

◄ **19.** The wood is placed on the work table, held with clamps. A scraper blade is passed over the surface in the direction of the grain, applying pressure until the entire surface is even. Then, it is sanded briskly with 150-grit sandpaper until the surface is smooth and polished.

▲ **20.** In this project, the finish consists of a coat of colorless wax, which highlights the color of the woods. The wax is applied with a cotton cloth.

► **21.** When the surface is dry, it is buffed with a cotton cloth. The result is a highly decorative piece of marquetry.

Veneering involves covering a support (made of inexpensive wood) with one or several layers of rich wood. The veneer is attached with glue, and pressure is applied to the surface. This technique adds a certain quality to furniture and objects whose structures are made of low-quality woods or have little aesthetic value. It differs from marquetry in that it uses veneer to make simple geometric designs, which result from the combination of sections of pieces arranged in different ways.

The Technique of Veneering

Veneering always requires some preparation, consisting of a thorough sanding of the support. This step is important because any roughness, speck, or uneven area is more evident when it is covered with the veneer.

The traditional technique of using hot animal glue to bond the veneer to the support and smoothing it with the veneer hammer is a time-consuming process that today is falling into disuse. The hot glue is being replaced with other vinyl adhesives that produce satisfactory results.

However, the technique descended directly from the systems used by the Egyptian and Roman civilizations to cover furniture with veneer made of precious metals, semiprecious stones, and exotic woods. Its use was abandoned during the Middle Ages, and it was not resumed until the arrival of the Renaissance in Italy. From the fifteenth century it was used along with marquetry to decorate furniture and interiors. With Europe's conquest of vast territories overseas, during the seventeenth and eighteenth centuries, new exotic woods that were appropriate for veneering were brought to the Continent. This period marked the peak for veneering. Today, because of the increasingly high cost of wood, the veneering technique has become industrialized.

Traditional Method

The traditional veneering process involves adhering veneer to a support, using glue of animal origin, and then applying pressure with a veneering hammer.

◄ **1.** In a metal container, the animal glue is covered with water and left to soak for 24 hours. Then it is heated in a double boiler until a paste of liquid consistency is created. (The glue should leave a sort of fine, continuous line when the brush is lifted.) A coat of hot glue is applied to the previously sanded wood surface that is to be veneered.

▲ **2.** Then, a layer of hot glue is applied to the underside of the veneer with a wide brush. The piece should always be slightly larger than the base to ensure that it will cover the surface of the wood. The excess veneer will later be removed with sandpaper or a knife.

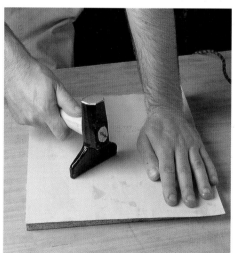

▲ **3.** The veneer is centered on the support and attached by applying pressure with a veneer hammer. The entire surface of the veneer is pressed by dragging the veneer hammer across it in a zigzag pattern while pressing on it. This step distributes the glue and removes any excess, while eliminating any bubbles that may have formed when the two surfaces were bonded.

◀ **4.** Because the veneer could warp when put in contact with the water-based glue, the surface should be wetted slightly. Tap water is applied with a handful of clean cotton strands.

▶ **5.** The bonding is activated by running a hot iron over the surface of the veneer. The evaporation of the water contained in the adhesive is speeded up by applying controlled heat.

Veneering with Double Sheets

With the veneering technique, similar veneers can be combined to create simple geometric forms or different veneers can be combined to create elaborate, more complicated forms. However, the most widely used designs are based on simple compositions. Double-sheet veneering is, together with book matching, the most simple design, which makes it the most appropriate for this technique.

▶ Countless designs and combinations can be made with the veneering technique. However, the designs most commonly used are based on simple arrangements, as can be seen in these examples: book match (a), double sheet (b), slip match (c), diamond match (d), reverse diamond match (e), and diamond match (f).

▶ **1.** The support is prepared with a thorough and brisk sanding done by hand using 150-grit sandpaper. Next, the center line is measured and marked on the wood: This is the line where the two veneer pieces will meet.

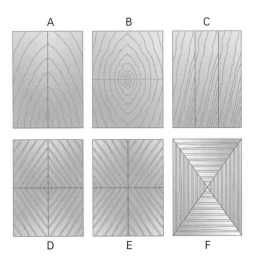

A   B   C

D   E   F

◀ **2.** Two consecutive sheets of veneer are selected from the package, in this case walnut, and checked to ensure that they are large enough for the base. They are attached (arranged in the same direction) on one of their sides with masking tape, which will prevent them from moving when they are cut. After measuring and marking the center line with a soft lead pencil, the veneer sheets are cut with a sharp knife or veneer saw. This task is carried out on a hard surface to prevent the veneer from getting scratched.

◄ **4.** The pieces of the composition are arranged on the board, with the seams along the centerline marked on the wood. One side of the veneer is attached to the support with masking tape, as a sort of hinge.

▲ **3.** One of the two sheets of veneer that were cut in half is selected, and the adhesive tape is removed. The top faces of the veneer are joined together and the grain lined up. They are attached with masking tape on their top faces. Then, the edges of the veneer are cut according to the dimensions of the support, leaving 3/8 inch (1 cm) extra as a precaution.

► **5.** White carpenter's glue (PVA) is diluted with water in a tray to make a liquid that is almost as fluid as water. The adhesive is applied to the wooden support with a roller.

► **6.** The veneer is attached to the wood by rotating it on the paper hinge. Next, the veneering hammer is used to press the veneer, dragging it in a zigzag motion to get a uniform and smooth surface. The veneer is lightly dampened with clean cotton strands soaked with tap water to prevent warping.

▼ **7.** Masking tape is applied to the free side as if it were a hinge. The veneer is placed between two wood boards slightly larger than the veneer. A sheet of newspaper or wax paper is inserted in between, to prevent any glue from adhering the veneer to the board. A press is made to size with wood pieces and attached with clamps.

▲ **8.** The piece is left in the press for 24 hours, while the PVA glue dries. After this time, the press is taken apart and the tape removed. Then, the surface is sanded (in this case with an orbital sander) with 150-grit sandpaper.

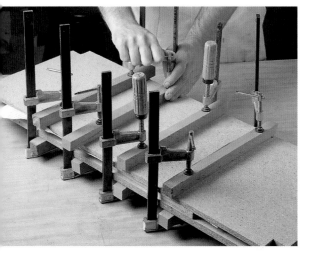

◄ **9.** A wood filler varnish and wax is used for the finish. The varnish is applied with cotton strands, until the pores are completely sealed. Gloves and a respirator are used for protection.

▲ **10.** When the surface is dry, it is sanded with 400-grit sandpaper, in the direction of the grain.

▲ **11.** Next, it is buffed with fine steel wool (number 0000) until any marks from the application of varnish are eliminated.

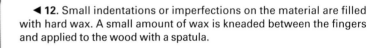

◄ **12.** Small indentations or imperfections on the material are filled with hard wax. A small amount of wax is kneaded between the fingers and applied to the wood with a spatula.

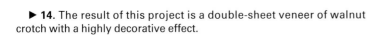

▲ **13.** Finally, a light tint is applied with a cotton cloth. When this dries, it is buffed with a clean cotton cloth.

► **14.** The result of this project is a double-sheet veneer of walnut crotch with a highly decorative effect.

Four-Piece Matching

Four leaves of veneer can be combined in two book arrangements and attached to each other to produce quite decorative effects. The technique is often used for veneering large surfaces, like tabletops, doors, and headboards, among others.

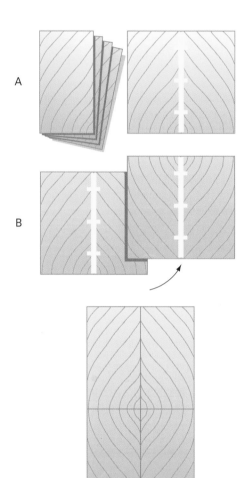

▲ This is the procedure used to veneer a surface with the four-piece matching technique. First, four consecutive veneer sheets are selected from the bundle. The first two are attached with masking tape on the top face as if they were the pages of a book (a); the grain should be aligned. Then, the edges are squared and cut. The same procedure is repeated with the two remaining sheets of veneer. They are book matched and attached, and the composition is rotated 180 degrees (b) so the four sheets of veneer are facing each other. Finally, both compositions are attached with masking tape, adjusting the sheets as needed to match the grain.

Diamond Matching

Several techniques are available for making diamond-matched veneer. This example explains how to make the pattern without any complicated steps. It involves transferring the measurements of each part of the support onto the veneer so the four rectangular pieces match perfectly together and fit on the wood base.

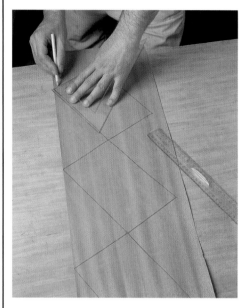

▼ 1. The wood is sanded thoroughly. The diamond design is formed by joining four rectangular pieces of veneer, each cut at a 45-degree angle. Then, the area on the base is divided into equal quarters and marked, to serve as a guide for cutting the veneer.

◄ 2. A piece of veneer with a straight, pronounced grain is chosen (in this case, embero), and the cutting lines are marked with a pencil. This provides four consecutive sheets of veneer whose grain will be perfectly matched, which will save material. To mark the veneer, one quarter section of the support (a rectangle) is measured and transferred to the veneer, first drawing the short sides diagonally to the grain of the wood. Then, the rest of the rectangle is marked by making one parallel line and one at 90 degrees. The rest of the pieces are marked the same way, measuring each quarter of the base and transferring the measurements to the veneer (numbering them). The angles should always be checked.

◄ 3. The veneer is placed on a hard surface and cut with a sharp knife. A ruler is used to ensure that the cuts are perfectly straight.

◄ 4. The procedure explained in the previous section (book matching) is followed. The pieces of veneer are neatly held together along the edge, with masking tape. The composition is attached to the base with masking tape as if it were a hinge, and it is fixed to the support with PVA glue applied with a roller.

5. The piece is placed in the workshop press, and it is left for 24 hours until the glue dries completely.

▶ **6.** When the piece is dry, the masking tape is removed. Because the piece is fragile, the tape should be removed gently, to prevent breakage or loss of material.

▲ **7.** Therefore, the surface is scraped with a scraper blade moving diagonally, until the masking tape is removed completely.

▲ **8.** Next, the surface is sanded with 150-grit sandpaper. Any loss of veneer is fixed with hard wax, which is kneaded in a small amount between the fingers and applied with a wooden spatula. Then, the surface is waxed and polished.

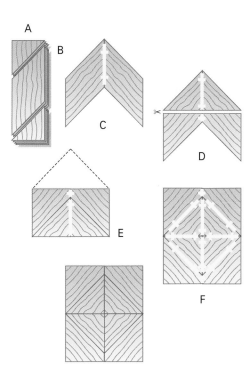

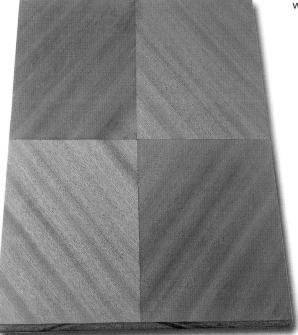

◀ **9.** The diamond shape veneer produces a peculiar effect, which changes according to the angle of the light.

Rhomboidal Matching

▲ This design also requires the use of veneer with straight grain. Four consecutive pieces of veneer from the same bundle are chosen and placed one on top of the other, in order (a). Next, the two ends are cut at a 45-degree angle (b). The top and bottom pieces of veneer are chosen. The top piece is turned over and attached to the other with masking tape to form an inverted "V" (c). A straight cut is made from corner to corner (d), and the point from the top is then inserted into the lower corner and attached with masking tape (e). The process is repeated with the other two pieces turned 180 degrees. Then, the entire composition is put together with masking tape (f).

Veneering Shapes

Different wood veneers can be combined to make a design. The most elaborate ones consist of complicated geometric patterns formed by many different pieces of veneer. The most simple techniques (like the one in the example) are those with a geometric motif that is not overly elaborate, like the triangle here made of sycamore, inserted in a background of sapele wood.

◀ **1.** The first step is to choose the veneers. In this case, the two chosen have different characteristics in terms of color (one light and the other dark) and grain (one without and the other with marked linear figure). Then, the wood support is sanded thoroughly. When this is done, the piece of veneer chosen for the motif is attached to a board with masking tape. The design is drawn directly on the underside of the veneer.

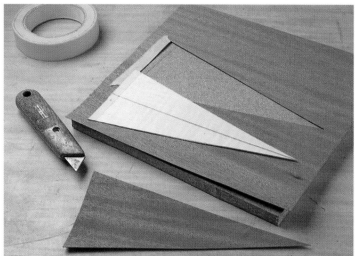

▲ **2.** The light veneer with the design is placed over the dark background veneer with masking tape. Then, they are cut with a sharp blade, using the ruler as a guide for straight and clean cuts.

▲ **3.** This process produces a shape that fits perfectly into the background veneer.

◀ **4.** The two pieces of veneer are attached (the triangle into the background) with gummed tape. The required length of tape is cut with scissors, and after wetting, it is glued to the veneer.

▼ **5.** The veneer is glued to the wood support (see the section on double-leaf veneering) and the piece is put into a press until the adhesive dries completely.

▶ **6.** The gummed tape is removed after it has been softened with a damp cotton cloth.

▲ **7.** Next, the paper is removed completely with a scraper blade following the direction of the grain.

◀ **8.** The project is concluded with a final sanding of the veneer and an application of shellac.

DECOUPAGE

The technique of decoupage (French word meaning cutout) involves decorating wood and by association, any surface, through the application of paper cutouts. This type of decoration requires anywhere from a single design to an infinite number of paper cutouts, which can be obtained from books and magazines or hand made. Once the motifs are selected and arranged on the wood, they are numbered and traced onto thin paper to make a pattern. This will serve as a guide, to make sure the result is identical to the one being planned. Next, each piece of paper is glued with the appropriate type of adhesive. Gum arabic is the one that produces the best results on paper. When this task is finished and the adhesive is dry, the paper (which is fragile by nature) is covered with a durable finish, like varnish or latex.

The Technique of Decoupage

Decoupage is an old technique that was widely used on popular and inexpensive furniture to imitate quality pieces adorned with painted decoration. The gluing of cards, prints, and colored drawings on the wood simulated painted decoration and marquetry, which were much more expensive. This art was popular during the seventeenth century in Italy, where it received the name of *arte povera* (poor art). Despite the name, the furniture decorated with this technique had a rich appearance, and the decorations were interesting. Decorating with decoupage continued to be used on popular furniture (Isabelline furniture) and its use has continued to this day.

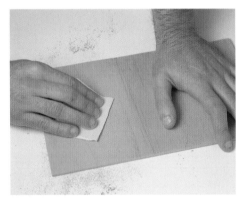

▲ **1.** The project begins with the preparation of the support. The wood is sanded with 150-grit sandpaper. It is essential to leave the surface smooth and free from imperfections, because any irregularity will be visible and will seem even larger when it is covered with paper.

▲ **2.** The larger motifs and those whose outline is somewhat irregular, with many protrusions, are cut using big, sharp scissors. To cut smaller motifs with more precision, a scalpel or a knife with interchangeable blades is used. The cutting is done on a hard surface (in this case a piece of plywood).

▲ **3.** Next, a sheet of tracing paper is cut to the same dimensions as the base. Then, it is placed over the wood and attached with masking tape to one of the sides, as if it were a book.

▲ **4.** Each cutout is lightly numbered on the back with a soft lead pencil so that it will not show through.

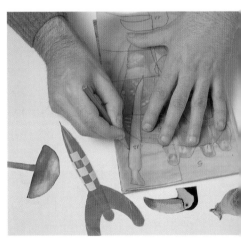

▲ **5.** The cutouts are placed on the wood and arranged into a suitable design. Then, the final arrangement is traced onto the paper using a pencil, drawing the outline of each cut out and its number, beginning with the larger ones and ending with the smallest one.

▲ **6.** The resulting pattern will serve as a guide for attaching each piece in its exact place.

▶ **7.** Next, the cutouts are glued to the support. First, gum arabic (the adhesive) is applied to the underside of the paper using the brush from the bottle.

▶ **8.** Then, following the pattern made on tracing paper, the cutout is placed in the exact position, guided by the outline and the numbers.

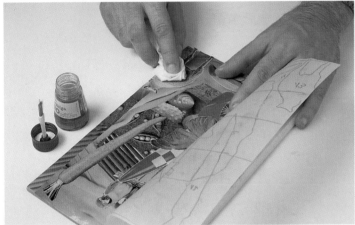

▲ **9.** Pressure is applied to the paper with a clean piece of cloth, to ensure that the piece has adhered well and to eliminate any traces of adhesive.

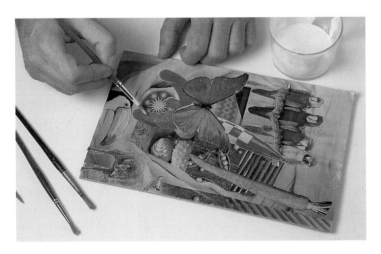

▲ **10.** When the gum arabic is dry, several generous coats of latex are applied with a badger-hair brush as a finish.

▶ **11.** The transparent latex finish protects and evens out the edges of the cutouts with the surface of the wood.

STAINING AND BLEACHING

*U*nlike the other techniques that have been covered so far, staining and bleaching are two processes that have only one thing in common—wood. They completely change the color of the wood without otherwise altering its exterior nature or appearance. The wood that is subjected to these treatments maintains the look of the grain, the figure, its original hardness, and so on; however it takes on a different color and tone. Staining colors the wood and bleaching removes the color, either restoring the original tone or making a lighter one. Products that restore color can bring tone and depth of the color back to wood that has suffered the aggression of time and weather, whereas protective products act as barriers to environmental agents (light and humidity).

Staining

Successful staining of wood depends on several factors. The first one is the type of wood being treated. Those woods with large amounts of tannin in their composition—like oak, chestnut, walnut, and mahogany, among others—are easy to stain and acquire an intense, deep color.

Another factor is the form or part of the wood being treated. The results of staining a solid board or piece of wood are different from staining plywood using the same procedure. The adhesive used to bond the veneer to the support can also alter the reaction of the stain.

The stain's solvent (water or alcohol) also affects the final result. Water-based stains evaporate evenly and produce an even finish, so they are ideal for large surfaces. Their tone can be darkened by applying several layers. The only problem is that the water raises the grain of the wood. To eliminate it, the surface must be scrubbed with a vegetable or esparto grass pad, because rubbing it with sandpaper would remove part of the applied color. Alcohol-based stains dry fast and do not raise the wood's grain. However, because the alcohol evaporates quickly, it is difficult to achieve an even finish without streaking. Normally, these stains are applied over large areas with a spray gun.

Before staining any type of wood, it must be thoroughly sanded to smooth the surface and free it from imperfections, and then it must be cleaned.

Natural Dyes

Natural dyes come from dissolving natural coloring agents, usually of vegetable origin, in water. To make them, a process of boiling and subsequent filtering (Brazil wood) or heating (logwood) is necessary. In every case, only small amounts of dye should be used, because of their high price and tendency to oxidize. The concentration of dye varies depending on the desired color and the wood that is to be stained. This is why the dye should be tested before the actual project is begun.

Chemical Dyes

Chemical dyes are produced by dissolving different proportions of chemicals in distilled water or alcohol. The use of distilled water ensures identical results every time the solution is mixed. If tap water is used, the results may vary depending on the concentration of chlorine and other components present in the water used to make it drinkable. Solutions are mixed hot to increase the power of the colorant and the penetrability of the dye. Water is heated to just below boiling, because any evaporation would cause the concentration to vary and the resulting color to change.

Fuming is a special type of coloring technique that relies on the oxidation power of ammonia vapors. It must be done in a sealed chamber (see illustration) outdoors or in a well-ventilated area. All metal elements should be removed from the object before being fumed, because the ammonia is corrosive and will damage the metal and stain the wood. It is possible to produce uneven patterns or geometric forms with this process. Areas that are not being colored can be masked off with wax, using a technique similar to batik on fabric.

Anilines are the least harmful chemical dyes. They are easy to use and economical, so they are often used in place of other chemical colorants. Aniline solutions in water are prepared hot and left to cool afterward. If they are prepared in large quantities, a little bleach is added to prevent any bacteria growth. Many colors are available, allowing an endless number of mixtures to be created.

Combinations of Natural and Chemical Dyes

The combination of natural and chemical dyes makes interesting and special results possible, as well as colors that are almost unique. The dyes are applied layer by layer over completely dry coats of dye. The order in which they are applied has no effect on the final color.

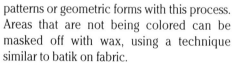

Staining

▶ **1.** The wood, an oak board, is thoroughly sanded: First, 100-grit sandpaper is used, then 150-grit sandpaper. The two consecutive sandings make the wood smooth, even, and free from imperfections and do not raise the grain.

◀ **2.** Because the board is dyed with various chemicals, the different surfaces to be dyed are separated with masking tape.

▶ **3.** The chemicals used for dyeing are heated (see the following pictures) in a microwave or in a double boiler. In both cases, it is important for the solution not to boil, because the evaporation of the water would cause changes in the concentration of the mixture and would alter the results.

▲ **4.** A solution of 10 percent iron sulfate ($FeSO_4$) in distilled water is prepared. While it is hot, it is applied evenly over the oak board, using a clean, wide brush. When the iron sulfate dries, it dyes the wood a dark, deep blue color.

▲ **5.** A potassium dichromate ($K_2Cr_2O_7$) solution is prepared following the previous proportions—that is, 10 percent of the product in distilled water. The mixture is heated, and then it is applied to the board.

◀ **6.** It is spread evenly with a clean, wide brush. The potassium dichromate produces an intense reddish brown color.

► **7.** The water-based dyes raise the grain of the wood. Rubbing the surface briskly with a vegetable scouring pad until it is completely polished prevents this from occurring.

▼ **8.** Lightly tinted furniture wax is applied with cotton strands or a cloth to protect the wood. When it is dry, it is polished by buffing it with a clean cotton cloth.

▼ **9.** The surfaces dyed with the iron sulfate (a) and the potassium dichromate (b) contrast with the central area of the board, which has not been stained but has been treated with wax because it was washed.

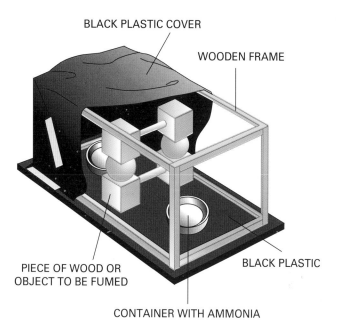

A   B

BLACK PLASTIC COVER

WOODEN FRAME

PIECE OF WOOD OR OBJECT TO BE FUMED

BLACK PLASTIC

CONTAINER WITH AMMONIA

Fuming

◄ A tightly sealed chamber for fuming the wood is made. This chamber consists of a heavy plastic base with a wooden frame and a plastic cover. The plastic should be completely opaque, preferably black, to protect the wood from the light, because its action would alter the result. The wood is placed inside with a ceramic or glass container holding some ammonia. When handling the ammonia, gloves and a respirator made for use with ammonia fumes should be worn. Next, all the seams in the plastic are tightly sealed with tape.

► After 5 minutes, the wood, which in this case is oak, acquires a dark honey color. Several coats of wax have been applied as a finish and polished. The difference is clear when compared with the un-treated oak board.

Cathedral Finish and Flemish Finish

▶ The **cathedral** finish (a) involves sealing the pores of a previously fumed surface with a mixture of powder pigments, linseed oil, and whiting; the mixture is wiped on with circular motions. The last coat should be applied following the direction of the grain, and when it dries it is polished with vegetable fibers and then waxed. The **Flemish** finish (b) involves applying asphalt heavily diluted with mineral spirits with cotton strands or a cloth to a surface that has been previously dyed with potassium dichromate.

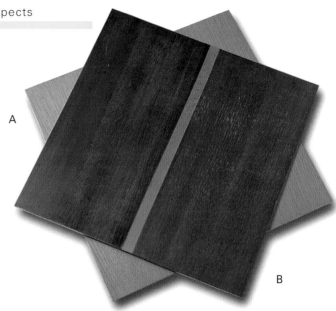

Aniline Dyes and Finishes

◀ Anilines always produce consistent results and stable colors. In this case, a maple board has been dyed with two aniline colors (a and b), leaving the center in its natural, untreated color.

White Grain Finish

◀ First, the wood is rubbed in the direction of the grain with a metal brush to open the pores. Then, the entire surface is thoroughly sanded. Next, a water-based aniline dye is applied, and when it dries, it is rubbed with vegetable fibers. Finally, a paste made of lithopone (a mixture of barium sulfate and zinc sulfur [$BaSO_4^+ZnS$]) and water is applied with vertical and horizontal movements. While the paste is still soft, the surface is rubbed with a vegetable pad to remove the excess. The surface must be protected with colorless wax.

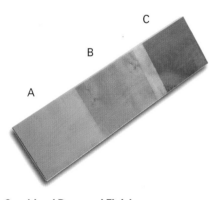

Combined Dyes and Finishes

▲ Maple is a type of wood that has no tannins, so dyeing it with natural products requires a mordant. Area A has been left untreated. Area B has been dyed with a solution of 10 percent tannic acid and distilled water, which was applied with a brush. When the surface was dry, a solution of logwood, also diluted in distilled water, was applied. Area C has been treated with a solution of 25 percent copper sulfate ($CuSO_4$) and water and left to dry. Then, it was painted with the solution of 10 percent tannic acid. When the surface was dry, a solution of logwood was applied.

▲ To dye a pine board (wood that, like all the conifers, has little tannin) two different methods are used. First, brazilwood is diluted in distilled water and brought to a boil. Then the liquid is strained through a finely knit cloth (a stocking). The dye is applied to part of the surface (a) using a thick brush. The rest of the surface (b) is dyed by first staining it with the brazilwood solution and then applying a solution of 10 percent iron sulfate ($FeSO_4$) and distilled water after the surface has dried.

▲ Another pine board is dyed, this time using different products. For the top part (a), a solution of 25 percent copper sulfate ($CuSO_4$) and distilled water is applied and left to dry. Next, the surface is painted with the logwood solution. The bottom part (b) has been painted in three layers, each being allowed to dry before the next application. The first coat is 10 percent potassium dichromate ($K_2Cr_2O_7$) and distilled water, the second one logwood, and the last tannic acid, also a 10 percent solution.

Bleaching

Hydrogen peroxide (H_2O_2) at a 30 percent solution and oxalic acid ($[COOH]_2$) in supersaturated solution with water are mainly used to bleach woods that have been dyed.

Hydrogen peroxide bleaches the wood by oxidizing and burning the surface, resulting in a whitish color. The wood must be allowed to dry completely to ensure the final results, because the tone can vary. If the resulting color or tone is not the desired one, the application should be repeated. In either case, the dry surface should be neutralized by rubbing it with cotton strands or a cloth soaked in tap water. Then, the surface should be rubbed with a vegetable pad or sanded, to remove the grain raised by the water.

Oxalic acid, a basic acid, is whitish and transparent and is often used in dry cleaning to whiten vegetable fibers. It is used in supersaturated solution (it precipitates at the bottom of the container) with water. When used on wood, it is applied with a brush and is then left to dry. Water from the solution evaporates during the drying period, and this causes minute crystals of oxalic acid to appear on the surface. They are eliminated by rinsing the surface with plenty of tap water. The process ends with a thorough sanding.

To bleach wood that has not been stained, sodium hypochlorite (common bleach) and hydrogen peroxide are used. Sodium hypochlorite bleaches gently, and its effect is visible after several applications. The result is a wood surface with a grayish, almost white, color. Hydrogen peroxide must be neutralized when it is dry, after arriving at the desired tone. The result is wood with a lighter color than the original.

Working with bleaching agents requires the use of protective gear like long neoprene gloves to cover the hands and forearms, a respirator, eye protection, and heavy clothing, preferably made of cotton.

How to Bleach Stained Wood Using Hydrogen Peroxide

◄ **1.** First, the wood surface is sanded thoroughly, using 150-grit sandpaper. Next, a 30 percent solution of hydrogen peroxide is applied with a wide brush to an area of the wood that has been stained.

► **2.** The surface is rubbed with cotton strands or cloth to remove some of the dye. These steps are repeated until a tone close to the one desired is achieved.

◄ **3.** When the wood is dry, the color is easier to see. If it is acceptable, the effect of the hydrogen peroxide is neutralized by rubbing the surface with a handful of cotton strands soaked with tap water. Then, the surface is sanded, to eliminate the grain raised by the water.

How to Bleach Stained Wood with Oxalic Acid

▼ **1.** A supersaturated solution of oxalic acid in tap water is prepared. It is supersaturated when part of the oxalic acid precipitates to the bottom of the container.

▲ **2.** A generous amount of the supersaturated solution is applied to the remaining area of the dyed wood.

◀ 4. A wad of cotton strands is soaked with water.

▲ 3. The wood is left to dry completely. Minute crystals of oxalic acid will appear on the surface, forming a powdery layer of a whitish color.

◀ 5. The wood is scrubbed with the wet strands until all traces of oxalic acid have been eliminated. After this, and once the wood is dry, the surface is sanded to remove the grain raised by the water.

A   B

▲ 6. Hydrogen peroxide (a) and oxalic acid (b) produce different results, even when applied to the same type of wood stained with identical products.

How to Bleach Natural Woods

▶ Sodium hypochlorite (common bleach) (a) and hydrogen peroxide (c) are applied to a piece of wood. Bleach produces a whitish gray tone, quite different from the untreated wood (b). Hydrogen peroxide makes the tone of the wood lighter.

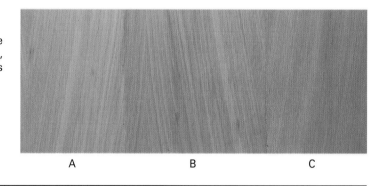

A   B   C

Products that Protect and Restore the Color

Protective products are used on exterior wood that is always exposed to the elements. They protect it without changing its appearance, producing a natural finish. Products made from synthetic resins are mainly used, because they penetrate the wood deeply and provide great resistance. The most common ones are latex and UV-resistant stains. This latter one is a synthetic resin that provides protection from ultraviolet rays, which cause the wood to age and darken. These stains are applied with a brush directly from the container or diluted in water, according to specific needs. Protective products should be reapplied every year, but in this case the wood does not need to be sanded first.

Color restorers are used to return the wood to its original color and tone. The one most commonly used is linseed oil. There are others made of mixtures of oils and waxes with tints that penetrate the wood without leaving a film or surface residue. They can be used directly from the container, but it is recommended that they be diluted with a small amount of mineral spirits or essence of turpentine, because this increases their ability to penetrate the wood.

▼ Linseed oil gives pine wood (a) a golden tone. UV-resistant finishes (b) have a filter that protects the wood from ultraviolet rays; when applied, these finishes leave a purplish white film that disappears with drying. Untreated pinewood (c).

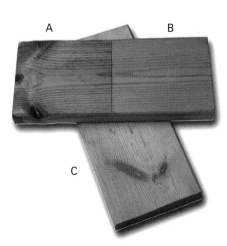

Safety

Certain basic rules of safety must be observed when handling dangerous tools and materials.

Before any material is used, the label, which indicates its composition, should be read. If it has a danger symbol, protective gear should be worn as required.

When handling a substance that is corrosive, an irritant, harmful, or toxic, neoprene gloves that are long enough to protect hands and arms should be worn. Disposable latex gloves are only useful for keeping hands clean. A respirator with interchangeable filters should be used as protection from the listed substances. Filters are sold separately from the masks, which allows them to be changed as appropriate, according to the substance being used. It is important to renew the supply of masks and filters regularly, to ensure that they do not exceed the expiration date or the required time of use recommended by the manufacturer. A mask or filter should never be tampered with to lengthen its use time. Disposable masks should be used only for a short time as protection from organic gases or dust. Eye protection prevents harm to the eyes.

Flammable or toxic products should be stored in a metal cabinet with a lock and far from any sources of heat. The containers, tightly sealed to avoid evaporation, should be positioned so that the toxicity symbols are visible upon opening the cabinet. Before any tool is handled for the first time, the instructions and recommendations of the manufacturer should be read carefully. Tools should be stored in their original box or bag, together with their refills and instructions for their use. The tools that are frequently used can be stored mounted on the wall so they can be seen.

Eye protection should be worn when sawing or when doing any type of work that produces large amounts of particles. The protective gear should be flexible and wide enough to fit comfortably, even when prescription glasses are worn. Disposable masks are the most comfortable ones to use as protection for tasks that produce dust, because they are light, easy to put on, and effective.

Clothing and footwear should always be comfortable, preferably made of natural fibers (cotton is the best), and stain resistant.

It is also recommended to have at least one fire extinguisher stored in an accessible location, with an updated maintenance inspection record. A first aid kit with a good assortment of products is also good to have, and it should be placed in a visible, easy-to-reach location.

RESPIRATOR AND FILTER CHART		
COLOR	TYPE	USE
	A	Organic vapors.
	AP	Organic vapors + dust.
	B	Inorganic acid gases.
	BP	Inorganic acid gases + smoke, and fumes.
	E	Sulfuric acid.
	EP	Sulfuric acid + dust, smoke and fumes.
	K	Ammonia.
	KP	Ammonia + dust, smoke, and fumes.
	AB	Organic vapors + inorganic acid gases.
	ABP	Organic vapors + dust, smoke, and fumes.
	P	Dust, smoke, and fumes.
	ABEK	All purpose filter for gases.
	ABEP	All purpose filter for gases and ammonia + dust, smoke, and fumes.
	ABEKP	All purpose filter for gases + dust, smoke, and fumes.

▲ Protective gear, like a respirator with interchangeable filters and long neoprene gloves, is required when working with toxic materials. Also, comfortable cotton clothing is recommended.

DANGER SYMBOLS AND THEIR MEANINGS

Explosive Substances		E	**Danger:**	This sign indicates substances that can explode under certain conditions.
			Precaution:	Avoid shock, impact, friction, sparks, and heat.
Combustible Substances		O	**Danger:**	Oxidizing compounds can ignite combustible substances or can help spread existing fires, making them more difficult to extinguish.
			Precaution:	Avoid any contact with combustible substances.
Extremely Inflammable Substances	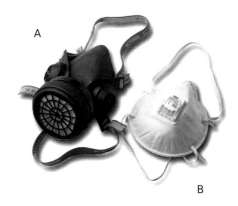	F+	**Danger:**	1. Liquids with a combustion point less than 32°F (0°C) and a boiling point less than 95°F (35°C).
			Precaution:	Avoid any contact with sources of ignition.
			Danger:	2. Gases and mixtures of gases (also liquid gases) that are easily ignited in the air.
			Precaution:	Avoid the formation of inflammable gas-air mixtures, and avoid sources that ignite them.
Easily Inflammable Substances		F	**Danger:**	1. Self-igniting substances. Substances that ignite when they come in contact with air.
			Precaution:	Avoid contact with air.
			Danger:	2. Substances sensitive to humidity. Chemicals that create inflammable fumes when they come in contact with water.
			Precaution:	Avoid contact with humidity and water.
			Danger:	3. Liquids with an ignition point below 70°F (21°C).
			Precaution:	Isolate the flames, heat sources, and sparks.
			Danger:	4. Solid substances that are easily ignited after short exposure to a source of ignition.
			Precaution:	Avoid all contact with sources of ignition.
Toxic and Very Toxic Substances		T T+	**Danger:**	These substances are harmful if inhaled or swallowed or if they come in contact with the skin; they may even cause death. Therefore, this symbol indicates the possibility of irreversible damage from a single, repeated, or short-time exposure.
			Precaution:	Avoid any bodily contact. In case of illness contact a doctor.
Harmful Substances		Xn	**Danger:**	These substances are harmful if inhaled or swallowed or if they come in contact with the skin. This symbol indicates the possibility of irreversible damage from a single, repeated, or short-time exposure.
			Precaution:	Avoid bodily contact with the substance as well as the inhalation of fumes. In case of illness, contact a doctor.
Corrosive Substances		C	**Danger:**	Living tissue and other materials are destroyed from contact with these substances.
			Precaution:	Do not inhale the fumes, and avoid contact with skin, eyes, and clothing.
Irritant Substances		Xi	**Danger:**	This symbol indicates those substances that can irritate the skin, the eyes, and the respiratory system.
			Precaution:	Do not inhale the fumes, and avoid contact with skin and eyes.
Substances That Are Harmful to the Environment		N	**Danger:**	Substances that over time can cause negative effects in the flora and fauna of any environment (aquatic or on land).
			Precaution:	Do not dispose of them in the environment.

▲ Protective eyewear.

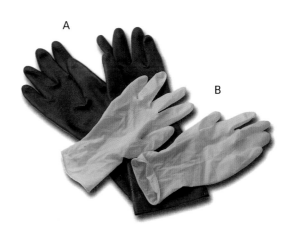

▲ Respirator with interchangeable filters for organic fumes (a), dust and smoke mask (b).

▲ Neoprene gloves (a), disposable latex gloves (b).

*T*his chapter consists of three practical exercises in which most of the processes explored in the previous chapter, "Technical Aspects," are covered. Two or more combined or complementary techniques are used in each exercise to create an attractive decorative object. Different decorative techniques and solutions have been chosen, depending on the piece, all of which are furniture. In every case, the decoration adds new aesthetic value to old or simple objects. The first exercise illustrates the transformation of an old rocking chair that has been left outside and exposed to the elements, yet whose structure is in good condition. The cross rails of the back rest have been gilded, and the rest of the frame has been painted. Glazing has been applied to the painted areas in a slightly different tone from the base coat of paint to add quality and depth. The finish consists of an application of a layer of antique glaze. The result of the exercise is a renovated piece that can be used again.

In the second exercise, the changes made to a simple tray made of inexpensive wood are explained. The base has been decorated using marquetry, which required a complex procedure to make a game board. The marquetry was applied to a board, which was then attached to the surface of the tray to strengthen it. The game pieces are made of solid wood inlaid with various materials. In this case, the decorative process has changed the use of the object: The serving tray has been transformed into a game table.

In the third exercise, the decoration of a commercially manufactured box is illustrated. The top of the lid has been veneered with a higher-quality, better-looking wood than the box is made of. The remaining surface of the object has been stained with a matching color that combines perfectly with the veneer. The pyrography technique has been used to create a geometric design on the veneer. The result of the decorative process is a unique piece—a box that is an attractive work of art, a far cry from the original mass-produced piece.

Step by
Step

Painted and Gilded Rocking Chair

*D*ecorative processes are often applied to old or damaged wood to give the piece a new aesthetic value, such as is the case here. In this exercise, the task is to decorate a rocking chair that has been left outside for an extended period. The wood is stained and has small superficial cracks; however, the general condition of the chair is good, and it is solid enough to be used. Given the imperfections in the surface of the wood, the decoration should cover the frame completely to conceal them.

The process begins with the preparation of the wood with several coats of primer, which both conceals the imperfections and serves as a base for the various techniques used. All parts of the chair have been painted, with the exception of the cross rails in the chair back, which have been gilded. The finish involves applying a glaze over the paint on the rocking chair, using colors in the same value range, and then antiquing the surface of the chair.

▼ This rocking chair was outside for an extended period, which caused stains, surface damage, and small cracks from the elements. To conceal the imperfections, the entire surface is decorated.

▲ 1. The work begins by applying masking tape to the corners where the seat joins the posts supporting the armrests, to prevent any staining and dripping.

► 2. The surface of the wood is briskly rubbed with coarse sandpaper.

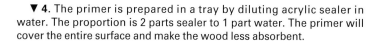

◀ **3.** The areas with the most damage, like the arms and parts of the base, are sanded repeatedly.

▼ **4.** The primer is prepared in a tray by diluting acrylic sealer in water. The proportion is 2 parts sealer to 1 part water. The primer will cover the entire surface and make the wood less absorbent.

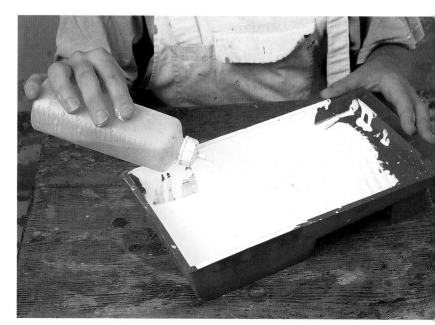

▲ **5.** The primer is applied with a number 20 natural-bristle brush to the corners and joints of the rocking chair.

▶ **6.** Then, the seat is covered with wrapping paper and tape to keep the woven esparto grass (which is in good condition) from getting stained.

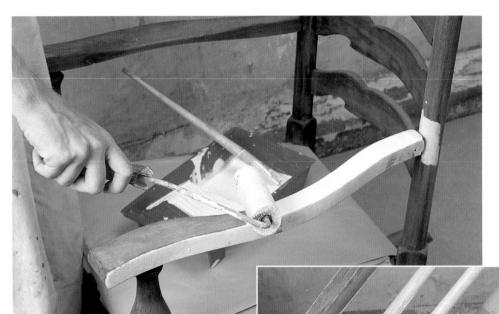

◀ **7.** The primer is applied with a roller to the flat surfaces, like the arms, the cross rails of the back and the base of the rocking chair.

▼ **8.** A coat of primer is applied with a number 20 natural-bristle brush to the turned pieces: the front chair legs and stretcher rail at the base of the chair. The entire surface of the wood must be covered, including the undersides.

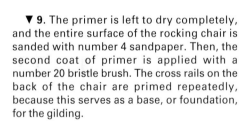

▼ **9.** The primer is left to dry completely, and the entire surface of the rocking chair is sanded with number 4 sandpaper. Then, the second coat of primer is applied with a number 20 bristle brush. The cross rails on the back of the chair are primed repeatedly, because this serves as a base, or foundation, for the gilding.

▶ **10.** When the second coat of primer is dry, all surfaces are briskly rubbed with a piece of 360-grit sandpaper, to help remove any traces of brush strokes and smooth out the corners and the edges.

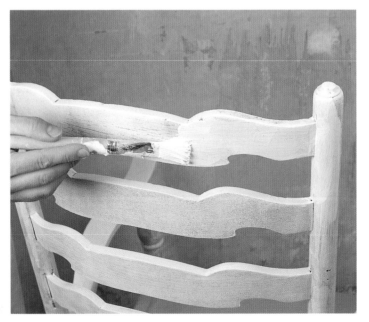

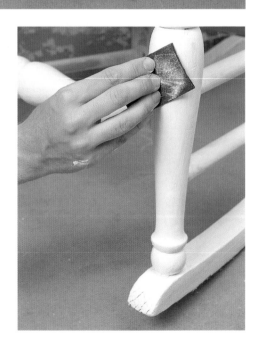

◄ **11.** The gilding procedure begins by applying a coat of shellac over the primer. To prepare the shellac, 4¹/₂ ounces (133 ml) of shellac flakes are poured into a glass jar.

▲ **12.** Then 8 ounces (250 ml) of 96 percent alcohol is added, and the jar is closed. The components are mixed by shaking the jar from time to time, until the shellac flakes have been completely dissolved. This process usually takes about 8 hours, so it is recommended that the jar be shaken every hour.

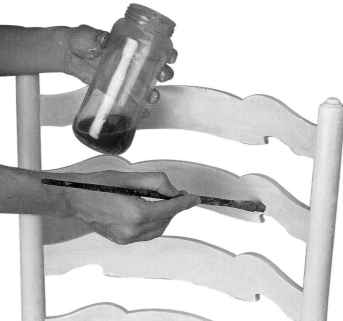

◄ **13.** A coat of shellac is applied to the cross rails of the backrest, using a flat brush made of soft sable hair or sabeline. The shellac should cover the primer completely, rendering the surface unabsorbent. This application requires a certain skill because it is important not to brush over the shellac, which could be dissolved by the alcohol in the brush and leave spots.

▼ **14.** While the coat of shellac dries, a thin layer of pastel yellow acrylic paint is applied to the rest of the surfaces of the rocking chair. Then the paint is left to dry completely.

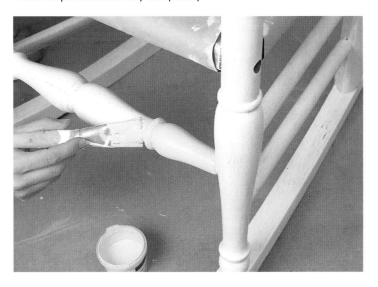

▲ **15.** In a plastic container, 4 parts white acrylic paint, 1 part tap water, and 2 parts latex paint are mixed. This amount should be sufficient to cover all surfaces of the rocking chair. The latex gives the paint transparency and the water thins it, which makes it easy to apply.

▲ **16.** A small amount of the mixture is separated and placed in a plastic container. A squirt of all-purpose blue stain and a few drops of black stain are added and mixed. However, caution is recommended with the stain: It is best to add a small amount and then increase it little by little until the desired tone has been achieved.

▶ **17.** The mixture is applied to the smaller areas using a number 20 natural-bristle brush. The arms, the base, and the lower legs of the rocking chair are painted.

◀ **18.** Before the layer of blue paint dries completely, the surface is rubbed with a clean cotton cloth to remove some of the paint and to allow the yellow paint to come through. This step should be done quickly because the latex paint has a short drying time.

▼ **19.** A portion of the first mixture is poured into a plastic container and tinted a salmon color, which is obtained by mixing a few drops of universal yellow tint with the same amount of universal red oxide. Again, color should be added in small amounts and increased little by little.

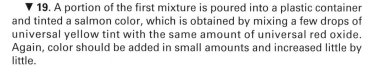

► **20.** The color is applied to small areas using a natural-bristle brush. It is spread over the parts of the rocking chair, alternating it with a cool color, in this case blue. The parts painted are the side stretcher bars, the turned elements of the legs, and the small details of the front stretcher bar.

► **21.** While the paint is still wet, the surface is rubbed with clean cotton strands or a cloth so the yellow of the base comes through.

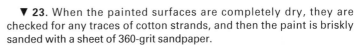
◄ **22.** The small details are painted with circular strokes in a clockwise direction, using a soft sable-hair brush. Then it is rubbed again with cotton strands.

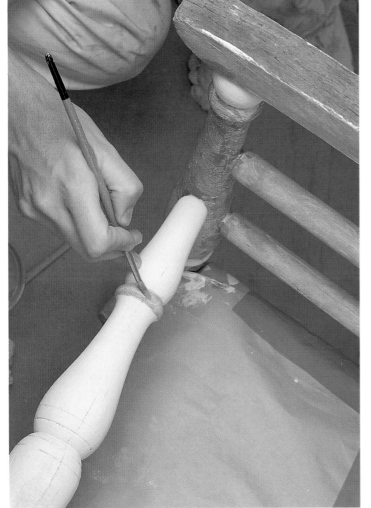

▼ **23.** When the painted surfaces are completely dry, they are checked for any traces of cotton strands, and then the paint is briskly sanded with a sheet of 360-grit sandpaper.

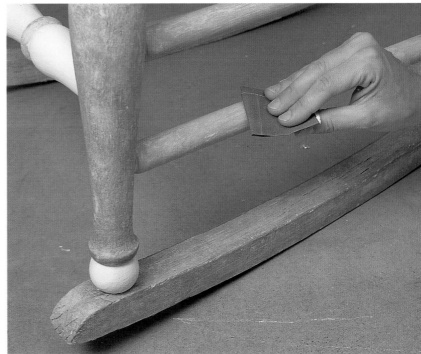

▲ 24. During this entire process the coat of shellac will have had a chance to dry. Now the crosspieces on the chair back are gilded. First, a substitute for the bole is prepared by mixing 3 ounces (90 ml) of liquid shellac with 2 tablespoons of red ochre powder pigment.

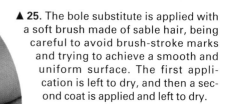

► 26. The gilder's tip is dampened with petroleum jelly to make picking up the gold leaf easier. To do this, a few drops of liquid petroleum jelly are placed on the back of the hand and then brushed with the gilder's tip.

▲ 25. The bole substitute is applied with a soft brush made of sable hair, being careful to avoid brush-stroke marks and trying to achieve a smooth and uniform surface. The first application is left to dry, and then a second coat is applied and left to dry.

▲ 27. A leaf of imitation gold is placed on the gilder's pad and a piece slightly larger than the surface to be gilded is cut off with a gilding knife and put aside. The surface of the leaf should always be larger than the area to cover because the leaves have to overlap all the edges to avoid any possible gaps at the seams.

► 28. A coat of mordant in water is applied over the bole substitute with a natural-bristle brush.

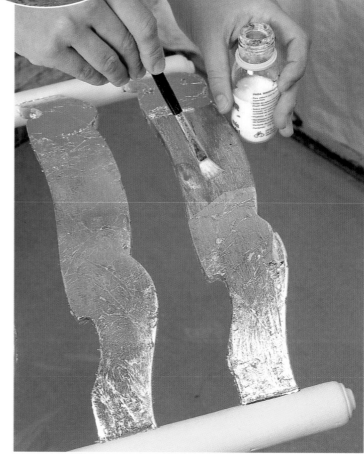

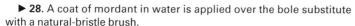

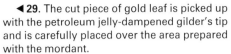

◄ 29. The cut piece of gold leaf is picked up with the petroleum jelly-dampened gilder's tip and is carefully placed over the area prepared with the mordant.

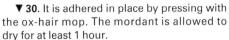

▼ 30. It is adhered in place by pressing with the ox-hair mop. The mordant is allowed to dry for at least 1 hour.

◄ 31. The surface is swept with a soft, wide brush made of sabeline to remove pieces of unglued gold leaf and any ragged edges.

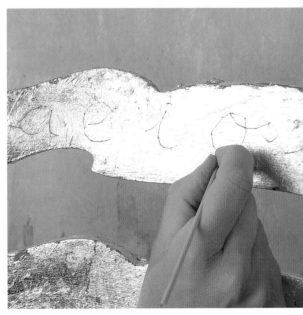

▲ 32. Several designs are incised in the surface of the gold leaf, using a wood stick with a fine point. The characteristic reddish color of the bole will come through.

▼ **33.** A small amount of linseed oil is mixed with a couple of drops of cobalt dryer. This mixture serves as a solvent base to make the antique glaze.

▶ **34.** A small amount of lemon-yellow oil paint is placed on a palette. A small portion of the solvent mixture is added with a natural-bristle brush to the oil paint until a fluid and transparent paste is formed. The paste is applied over the yellow painted areas.

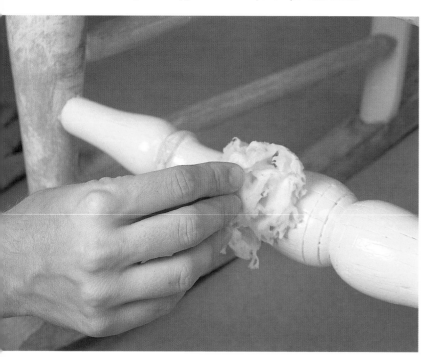

▲ **35.** The glaze is textured by lightly tapping the surface of the still-wet paint with a natural sponge.

▶ **36.** The process described here is repeated, mixing the linseed oil and dryer with blue oil paint.

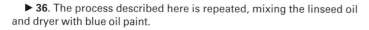

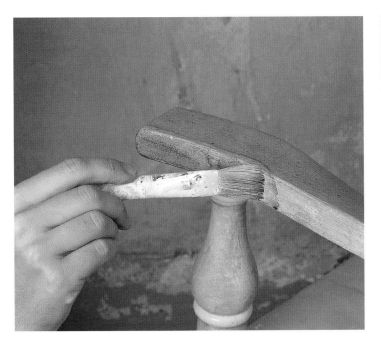

▲ **37.** The glaze is applied to the blue surfaces and tapped lightly with a natural sponge.

▲ **38.** The linseed oil and cobalt dryer are mixed with red oil paint.

▲ **39.** The red glaze is applied over the areas painted in salmon and tapped with a natural sponge. Because the linseed oil dries slowly, the glaze will have to be left to dry for at least 24 hours.

▶ **40.** After enough time has passed, the aging process begins. The edges and corners of the rocking chair are rubbed with number 000 steel wool to remove the paint. This way, the yellow color of the base or the coat of primer is revealed to create the desired affect.

◄ 41. The edges of the cross rails on the back of the chair are also rubbed to remove small areas of gold leaf. This way the characteristic reddish color of the bole will come through. This process gives the chair a used look and creates interesting color contrasts.

▲ 42. The gilded back stands out from the rest of the antiqued surfaces. A glaze is applied to dull the sheen and to give depth to the surface covered with gold leaf. To do this, enough liquid shellac to cover the entire surface is mixed with a small amount of red alcohol-soluble aniline powder. (The quantity depends on the desired intensity of the tone.)

► 43. The glaze is applied with a soft-hair brush, trying not to overlap the brush strokes.

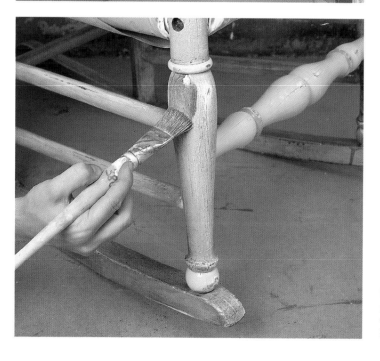

▲ 44. The process is completed by applying a mixture of protective varnish, made from 2 parts of glossy synthetic varnish, 1 part linseed oil, a couple of drops of cobalt dryer, and a small amount of raw umber oil paint.

◄ 45. The mixture is applied to the painted surfaces with a natural-bristle brush.

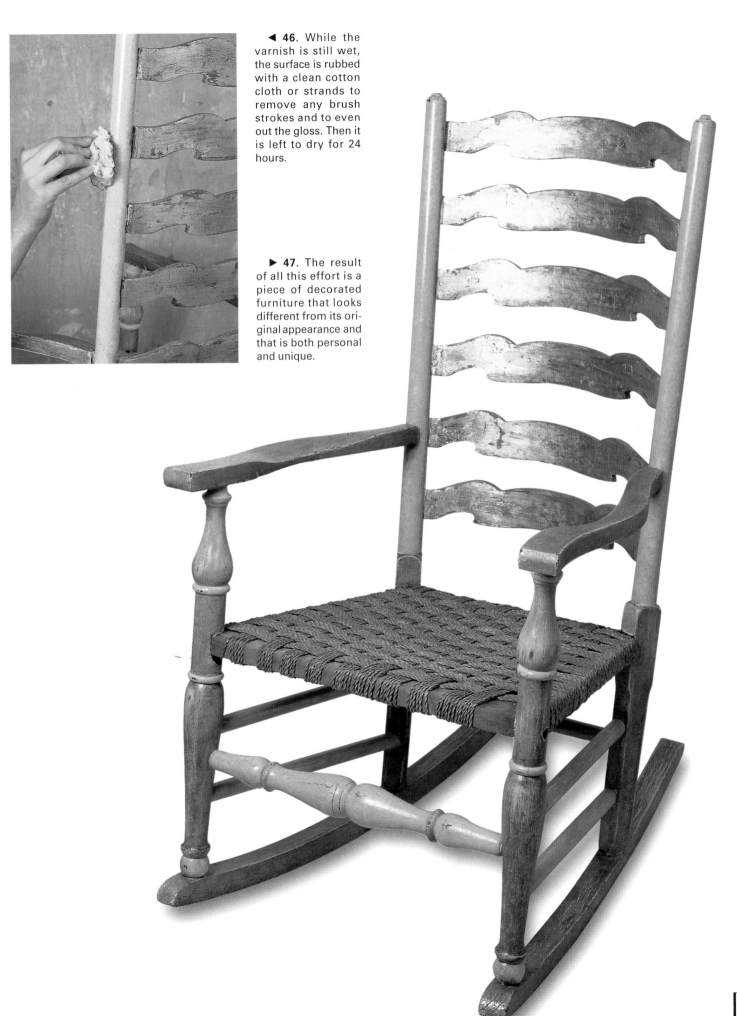

◄ **46**. While the varnish is still wet, the surface is rubbed with a clean cotton cloth or strands to remove any brush strokes and to even out the gloss. Then it is left to dry for 24 hours.

► **47**. The result of all this effort is a piece of decorated furniture that looks different from its original appearance and that is both personal and unique.

135

Tray with Marquetry and Inlay Work

*D*ecoration can also be a means of partially or completely transforming an object and altering its practical use. In this exercise, a tray of inferior quality, made with a thin sheet of wood, is turned into a game board that can also double as a serving tray.

   The board is decorated with marquetry, combining different kinds of wood veneer. Once the marquetry design has been assembled, it is attached to a medium-density fiberboard (MDF), which is then glued to the thin bottom of the tray, thus making it more substantial. The game pieces (tic tac toe) are made of rich materials like ebony and ivory, inlaid in solid walnut wood. These pieces contribute to the richness of the work.

◄ Here, a simply constructed tray is decorated. The base is made of a thin sheet of wood, which is quite worn.

▶ **1.** First, the wood veneer is chosen for the project—sapele and mukale. Then, the base of the tray is measured and the composition for the marquetry decided. In this case, a square board for the game tic tac toe will be created, and it will be framed with red rectangular strips that will cover the entire surface.

▼ **2.** The piece of sapele veneer is measured and marked. Because the veneer is narrow, a sharp knife is used to cut two rectangular pieces, which will form the middle square. The two veneer pieces are somewhat larger than the final board.

▼ **3.** The cut pieces of veneer are laid on a wood base and joined together on the underside with masking tape, which will be concealed when the procedure is finished. Special attention should be given to the direction of the grain and to the surface.

► **4.** A piece of mukale veneer is cut to a size similar to the previous piece. Then, hot rabbit skin glue is prepared in a double boiler: 2 parts rabbit skin glue granules to 1 part tap water, covering the granules. A sheet of newsprint is glued with this mixture to each piece of veneer,

for protection and reinforcement. The paper is attached to the face of the veneer that will be visible when the procedure is finished.

► **5.** The two veneer pieces are placed between sheets of paper and two Formica-covered boards, holding them under pressure with clamps. The glue should have a chance to dry completely—that is, for at least 24 hours.

◄ **6.** After the drying time is over, the press is taken apart and the masking tape carefully removed.

◄ **7.** On a sheet of white paper, a game board is copied or a custom design is made. Next, a piece of veneer of any type is cut to the same dimensions as the paper. Hot, liquid rabbit skin glue is spread over it with a wide brush, and it is glued to a piece of newsprint.

► **8.** A new coat of glue is applied over the newsprint, and the white paper with the design is glued to it. Then, the pressure is applied the same as before. It is left to dry for 24 hours.

▲ 9. The pieces of sapele and mukale veneer are joined together by applying masking tape around all of the edges to make a packet. The sheets of veneer are arranged in the same direction—that is, with the surfaces protected by the paper facing down.

▲ 10. The press is taken apart and the veneer with the game board design glued to it is removed. The design is measured and centered on the veneer package and attached with masking tape around the edges. Finally, the excess veneer is cut off, and masking tape is applied to all the sides.

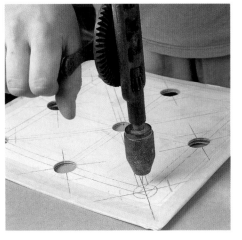

◄ 11. The cutting begins with the nine circles of the game board. A small hole is made with the hand drill held perfectly vertical, using a 3/64 inch (1 mm) bit, to make the insertion of the fret saw blade easier.

▼ 12. The saw blade is carefully passed through the hole, and the ends are attached to the frame by tightening the thumbscrews.

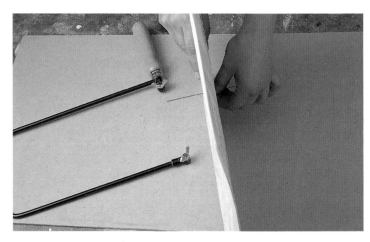

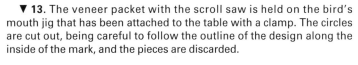

▼ 13. The veneer packet with the scroll saw is held on the bird's mouth jig that has been attached to the table with a clamp. The circles are cut out, being careful to follow the outline of the design along the inside of the mark, and the pieces are discarded.

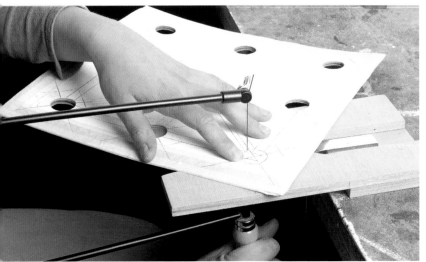

► 14. The inside of the nine circles is made with veneer that is different from the previous ones, in this case walnut. The first step in making them is to use a pencil and a circle template to trace circles identical to those of the game board onto white paper.

▲ **15.** Hot rabbit skin glue is applied to a piece of any kind of veneer, and the template is glued to it. This step will give body and stiffness to the paper with the design.

▲ **16.** Next, a strip is cut out of the walnut veneer. Hot rabbit skin glue is spread with a wide brush over the side that will be visible when the project is finished, and a sheet of newsprint is attached to it. Next, the two pieces of veneer are put in the press just as explained before, inserting sheets of paper in between to prevent them from adhering to each other.

▶ **17.** After 24 hours, the press is taken apart and the two pieces of veneer are put together to form a packet with masking tape around the edges.

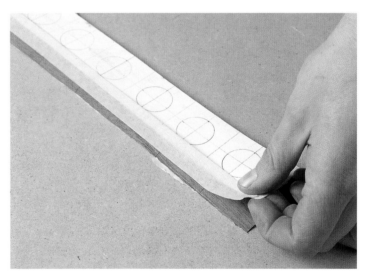

▼ **18.** The strip is set on a wood base, and pieces with the circles are cut out with a sharp blade. Both sides where the veneer was cut apart are covered with masking tape to prevent the veneer pieces from moving.

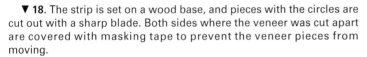

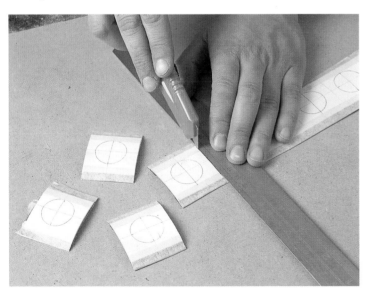

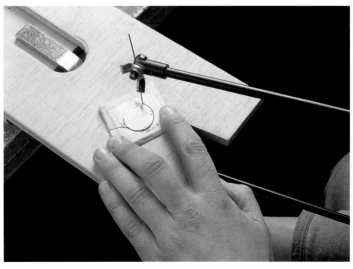

▶ **19.** Finally, the veneer packet is set on the bird's mouth jig attached to the work table. The circles are cut out and put aside. In this case, they are cut following the outside of the pencil line.

◀ **20.** The packet of veneer that has the design of the board game is placed on a wood board, and all the pieces are cut out. The cuts are made using a sharp blade and are guided by a metal ruler to guarantee perfectly straight lines. Furthermore, after each piece is cut out, it should be placed on the work table in front of the cutting surface, in the same position it was on the board. It is of the utmost importance never to change the order of the pieces, or the entire project could be ruined.

◀ **21.** The resulting cut pieces form the central area of the board, and two pieces of veneer could be used for the background. The veneer with the white paper is discarded. One of the background veneers is chosen, in this case the sapele, which dictates the color arrangement of the board.

◀ **22.** The top pieces covered with white paper are separated from the composition laid out on the work table and are discarded. The remaining pieces are picked up one by one, lifting them with a needle and arranging them in order on wood bases. The result is two compositions that repeat each other, one positive and one negative. The one with the sapele veneer as background is chosen, and the pieces are placed with the paper facing up.

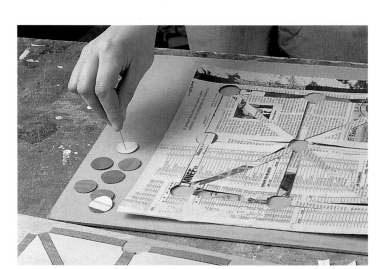

▶ **23.** The previously cut circles of walnut veneer are lifted with a needle and are carefully inserted into the empty spaces, with the paper facing up.

◀ **24.** A piece of packing paper is cut slightly larger than the composition, and hot rabbit skin glue is spread over one side.

▶ **25.** It is then glued to the composition to hold all of the pieces in place.

◄ **26.** The marquetry is immediately turned over, correcting any possible misalignments by moving the pieces with a needle. It is important to perform this task rapidly because the veneer tends to warp in a short time because of the water content of the glue.

► **27.** Next, the marquetry work is placed between two sheets of newsprint and placed in the press as previously explained.

► **28.** After 24 hours, the marquetry design is removed from the press. Four pieces of the mukale veneer are cut to the size needed to cover the rest of the bottom of the tray. They are attached to the marquetry design with masking tape.

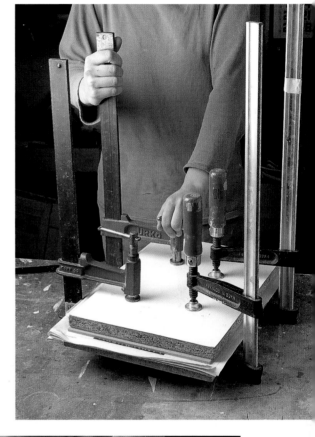

▼ **29.** Because the base of the tray is thin, the marquetry design is attached to a medium-density fiberboard (MDF), which is then glued to the bottom of the tray. The MDF is prepared by sanding the entire surface thoroughly with 100-grit sandpaper. Next, a coat of hot rabbit skin glue is applied with a wide brush, and the marquetry work is attached and put into the press, following the previously explained procedure.

▲ **30.** When the glue dries after 24 hours, the different layers of protective paper are removed from the surface of the marquetry. The paper is softened, lightly applying tap water with a clean cotton cloth, and then removed using a blunt scraper. Then the surface of the marquetry is left to dry completely.

▲ **31.** A sheet of 150-grit paper is used to sand the surface until it is flat and smooth to the touch.

▲ **32.** Excess material is removed and the edges rounded with a plane, making sure that the MDF fits perfectly over the base and between the sides of the tray.

► **33.** The board and the base of the tray are glued together with white carpenter's glue (polyvinyl acetate, or PVA) and placed in the press for 24 hours.

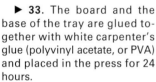

▼ **34.** Ivory and ebony are inlaid in solid walnut to make the six markers for the game. They should be the same diameter as the walnut circles on the board and the ivory and ebony pieces a little smaller. A circle template is used to mark the cutting line drawing directly on the ivory and the ebony, using the circle located before the one used for the board.

▼ **35.** The pieces are cut out with a fret saw, resting them on the bird's mouth jig attached to the work table.

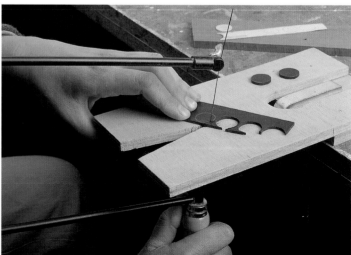

▲ **36.** To make a perfect circle and to remove any saw marks, the edges of the ebony pieces are rubbed briskly on a piece of coarse-grit sandpaper, attached to a wood base to make the task easier.

▲ **37.** The ivory pieces are worked for the same reason with a metal file, because ivory is a harder material.

◄ **38.** Using the circle template, the outside line (where it will be cut) is marked directly on the solid walnut piece, which should be the same diameter as the circles on the board. And the outside contour (which will be routed out) is also marked and should coincide with the ebony and ivory pieces. The center is marked with a gimlet.

▼ **39.** The walnut piece is attached to the work table with clamps. The exact size and shape is bored with the hand drill fitted with a centering bit, whose point is inserted in the hole made with the gimlet.

▼ **40.** A little more wood is removed with the chisel, making the holes deeper.

▲ **41.** Each piece is matched with a hole and the pairs are marked with the same number to avoid mixing them up. Next, hot rabbit skin glue is applied to the walnut, and each piece is inserted in its place.

▶ **42.** The surface of the inlay is protected with a piece of newsprint, and the piece is clamped as described before. After 24 hours, the press is taken apart and the piece removed.

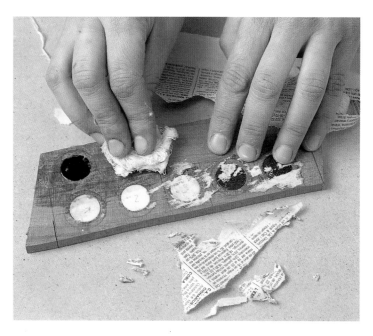

◀ **43.** The glued paper is removed by rubbing it with a clean cotton cloth soaked with tap water.

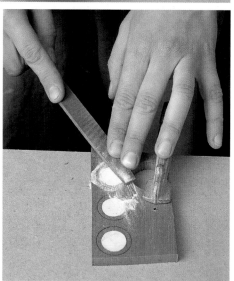

▶ **44.** When the surface of the wood is dry, the ivory pieces are made level with the walnut base. To do this, the surface of the piece is worked thoroughly with a file.

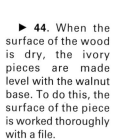

◀ **45.** The solid walnut piece is placed on the jig attached to the work table, and the markers are cut out following the outside pencil line with a fret saw.

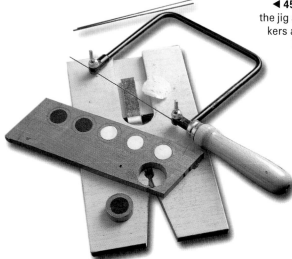

▶ **46.** The surface of the ebony piece is rubbed with a piece of coarse sandpaper attached to a wood base, using circular motions, to make it even with the solid walnut.

▲ **47.** The saw marks are removed by polishing the edges of the six pieces on a piece of sandpaper.

▲ **48.** Several coats of commercial matte varnish are applied with a wide brush to protect the board, the pieces, and the sides of the tray.

▶ **49.** The end result is an attractive object whose original practical use has been transformed. The richness of the woods used and the formal simplicity of the outcome has also added great aesthetic value.

Stained Box with Veneer and Pyrography Decoration

*M*ass-produced wood objects lend themselves to decoration and result in unique and special pieces that are far more attractive than factory-made pieces. In this case a box made of plain wood with simple lines has been transformed into a richly decorated object. A combination of techniques has been used to carry out the project. The entire surface of the lid has been covered with two types of veneer, which creates a color contrast. Then, a star motif has been burned into the central veneer using pyrography. The sides, the bottom, and the inside have been stained with a color coordinated with the veneer pieces, which allows the original grain of the wood to show through. This highlights the decoration of the most important part of the object— the lid.

◄ The object to be decorated is a mass-produced, unvarnished, pine box, which can be bought in any craft store. The surface and the finish are simple.

► **1.** The first step involves sanding the surface of the wood thoroughly. The piece is rubbed briskly with 100-grit sandpaper until a flat and smooth surface is achieved, free from roughness or any uneven areas.

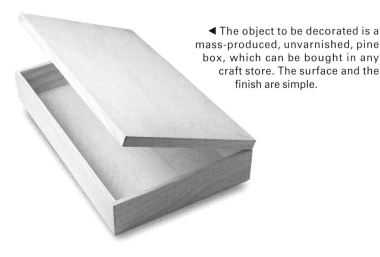

◄**2.** The decoration consists of a central piece of veneer framed by others of different woods around it. To begin, the edges of the veneer pieces are marked directly on the lid with a pencil, using a metal ruler as a guide and a triangle to mark the mitered corners.

▼ **3.** After the areas have been laid out, each part that forms the frame is numbered.

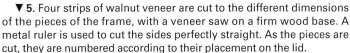

◄ 4. Walnut veneer is chosen for the frame surrounding the central piece of veneer. Before cutting, the top face of the veneer (the one that will be visible when the process is finished) is protected with paper. Gummed paper tape is used for this. After wetting it lightly with tap water, it is attached to the veneer, completely covering the area that is to be cut.

▼ 5. Four strips of walnut veneer are cut to the different dimensions of the pieces of the frame, with a veneer saw on a firm wood base. A metal ruler is used to cut the sides perfectly straight. As the pieces are cut, they are numbered according to their placement on the lid.

▲ 6. The paper tape protects the edges of the strips and keeps them smooth; without it the veneer could have been cracked or broken because it was cut across the direction of the grain.

► 7. Sycamore veneer is chosen for center of the lid because the grain and color of this wood contrast with that of the walnut. First, the shape is marked directly on the veneer with a pencil, making sure that the dimensions coincide with the area of the lid. Then, it is cut along the lines with a sharp blade on a wood surface, using a metal ruler as a guide.

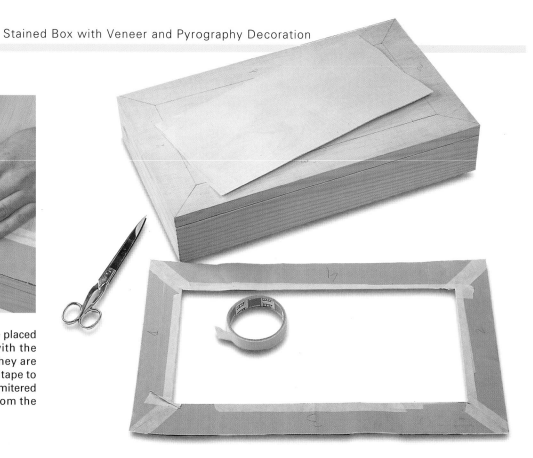

▲ **8.** The strips of walnut veneer are placed on the lid matching the numbers with the paper-covered surfaces facing up. They are attached to the surface with masking tape to prevent them from moving. Next, the mitered corners are marked with a pencil, from the outside corner to the inside corner.

▲ **9.** They are attached together with masking tape to form a frame and cut along the pencil mark with a sharp blade. This way, the mitered cuts will fit perfectly. Next, they are reattached with masking tape.

◄ **10.** The walnut veneer frame whose top face is still covered with paper is put back on the lid, and one of its long sides is attached to the side of the box with masking tape, as if it were a hinge.

► **11.** Next, the sycamore veneer, with the side that will be visible when the process is complete facing up, is attached to the walnut frame with masking tape. This way the composition can be inspected before the pieces are glued on.

◀ **12.** White carpenter's glue (PVA, or polyvinyl acetate) is poured into a container and diluted with tap water until a fluid liquid is made. The consistency of the glue varies depending on the brand and the length of time since the container was first opened. Therefore the amount of water that has to be added also varies. However, it is common practice to make a solution of 1 part glue to 1 part water. Next, the glue is spread evenly on the box using a roller.

▶ **13.** The veneer assembly is placed on the lid, using the masking tape hinge as a guide. The box is held between solid wood boards, protecting the lid with several sheets of newsprint. Several strips of wood are laid across the boards and clamped tightly at their ends to the ends of the wood boards to apply pressure to the veneer. The glue is left to dry completely for at least 24 hours, and after that time the press is taken apart.

▼ **14.** The dye that will be used to stain the sides, bottom, and inside is prepared. This is done by putting enough tap water to completely cover the outside and inside faces of the box in a container and heating it on an electric hot plate. Once the water is hot, but not boiling, a small amount of water-soluble orange aniline powder is added.

▼ **15.** The mixture is stirred with a wooden stick until the solution is completely diluted. The stain is tested on a piece of wood similar to that of the box and the result is compared with the veneer frame. The color can be made lighter or darker by adding either water or aniline.

◄ **16.** The lid is removed from the rest of the box by unscrewing the hinges. Next, the water-based aniline dye is applied with a wide brush. Latex gloves are used to protect the hands.

► **17.** When the surface of the wood is dry, the grain that has been raised with the water is eliminated. The surface is briskly rubbed in the direction of the grain with vegetable fibers or a brush.

▼ **18.** The protective paper is removed from the veneer, first softening it by rubbing it lightly with clean cotton strands or a cloth saturated with tap water. Then it is peeled off using a scraper blade, a chisel, or both.

▲ **19.** When the veneer is dry, the entire surface is thoroughly sanded in the direction of the grain of the wood, using 150-grit sandpaper.

◄ **20.** The edges of the lid, where the veneer meets the frame, are sanded with the same sandpaper until they are rounded and smooth and the area where they meet can barely be noticed.

► **21.** The design that will be burned on the center of the lid is draw on a piece of paper. An eight-pointed star has been chosen for this project

► **22.** Next, the design is copied with a pencil onto tracing paper.

◄ **23.** It is very important to center the design; otherwise the project could be ruined. Therefore, the sycamore veneer is measured, and the center point is marked with a pencil.

▼ **24.** The design is checked again with a triangle with graduated markings, to ensure it is square and centered. Next, the tracing paper is attached to the veneer with masking tape to prevent it from moving.

▼ **25.** The design is traced directly onto the sycamore veneer, pressing hard with the pencil while going over the lines.

▲ **26.** When the tracing is finished, the lines of the design are retraced with an awl guided by a metal try square to ensure straight lines.

▲ **27.** The lines of the star are carefully drawn with the wood-burning iron set on medium heat. Then, the sides of the lid are stained and sanded, and the lid is attached to the body of the box.

▲ **28.** The finishing of the box begins with the application of a wood filler over the entire surface, in several light coats, using a few cotton strands or a cloth. It is necessary to use gloves and a respirator for fumes.

▲ **29.** The wood filler dries quickly, so the entire surface is immediately sanded with 400-grit sandpaper, which removes any marks. The sanded surface has a characteristic whitish appearance.

◄ **30.** The surface is rubbed with a 0000 steel wool pad, which completely removes any marks left by the previous sanding.

▶ **31.** A coat of tinted furniture wax is applied with cotton strands or a pad. When it is dry, the surface is buffed by briskly polishing with a clean cotton cloth until a satiny gloss is obtained.

▼ **32.** The end result is a special object that is personal and unique—and that is completely different from the original mass-produced box.

Glossary

a

Acetate. A transparent material that is used to make photographic film.

Acrylic. Varnish or paint whose medium is a mixture of vinyl and acrylic compounds.

Adhesive. A substance that is used to bond two surfaces. Depending on its origin it can be synthetic, mineral, animal (glue), or vegetable (gum).

Alkaline. A substance that counteracts the effects of acids. It is also known as base.

Aniline. A generic name for pigments derived from organic synthesis. They make colorful, transparent dyes.

Asphalt. A substance made from the mixture of hydrocarbons dissolved in oil and solvents. It is used mainly for aging patinas and restoring wood because it produces a warm brown color that is appropriate for detailing and glazing.

Awl. A tool with a long, pointed metal rod and a wooden handle. It is used to bore holes, to draw on surfaces, and to pick up small pieces of wood or other materials.

b

Band. Veneer strip.

Beating. A technique for working certain metals like gold and copper that involves striking them with a hammer until they form thin sheets.

Binder. A substance that is mixed with pigments to bond the particles together to make paint.

Bleach (to). To modify color, by making a tone lighter, or to remove the color of the wood through the application of chemicals.

Bole. A mixture of natural iron oxide, clay, calcium silicate, and magnesium. It is orange in color and is used as a mordant base for water gilding. Nowadays synthetic mixtures are often substituted.

Burnish (to). To shine a gilded or waxed surface by buffing with either a burnisher or cotton cloth. Burnishing makes the surface smooth and gives it a deep, satiny gloss.

Burnisher. A tool with a smooth and rounded hard stone (normally agate) attached to a metal tip with a wooden handle. It is used for burnishing gilded surfaces.

Burr. Part of the edge of a scraper blade that stands out and that is used to remove material by scraping.

Butt joint. Two boards or pieces of wood attached together without the use of joints.

c

Casein. A protein that separates from milk when it curdles. It is then processed to make it water soluble and used as a binder for paint.

Chamois. Cured thin sheepskin, usually of lesser quality.

Chisel. A tool that has a steel blade with a wide and flat cutting edge and a wooden handle. It is used for carving wood.

Clamp. A plastic or metal tool used to hold two pieces of glued wood together so they completely bond to one another.

Coloring agent. Colored substance that can be applied to certain materials to give them color or to dye them.

Color saturation. When the color is of the highest intensity and purity.

Comb. A tool with a handle holding several square teeth. It is used in different decorative techniques to make designs by removing paint to imitate the grain of the wood.

Crotch. Fork in the trunk of a tree, where branches grow.

Cutting gauge. A tool that is similar to the marking gauge fitted with a small cutting blade at one end. It is used for cutting veneer strips and for deeply marking the wood.

d

Decant (to). To slowly pour part of the liquid of a mixture, controlling the amount, to prevent the sediment or the substance on the bottom from coming out.

Diffuser. A tool with a round rubber or foam head and a wooden handle. It is used in certain decorative techniques to diffuse the grain.

Dragging brush. A wide brush with long hair that is used in certain decorative techniques to give the paint texture.

e

Earth colors. Generic name for brown, ochre, and yellow tone pigments of mineral origin.

Emulsifier. A substance, generally oil based, that is added to a water-based substance to produce an emulsion.

Emulsion. A mixture of liquids or solids in liquids in which particles or drops remain in suspension because the substances are nonsoluble.

Enamel. Commercial paint made with an oil or plastic varnish and finely crushed pigments that makes the surface shiny and smooth when it dries.

Essence of turpentine. Purified turpentine that is used as a solvent or as a medium in oil techniques.

f

Felt. Heavy cloth made of wool or other nonwoven materials; its fibers are intertwined and adhere to one another.

Fret saw. A tool with a fine blade and sharp teeth, mounted vertically in a metal frame. It is used for sawing marquetry.

Fuming. Coloring technique for certain types of woods (especially oak) that involves placing the object in an environment that is saturated with ammonia vapors.

Fuzz. A group of fibers on the surface of the wood that are raised in a direction opposite to the normal one. The grain of the wood is raised when it is wet.

g

Gesso. This word comes from the Italian *gesso* (gypsum), although the material bears no relationship with this term. It is a commercial product made with a plastic emulsion binder and gypsum, chalk, or similar materials. It is used for priming.

Gilder's pad. A tool with a rectangular piece of wood covered with chamois, for holding metal leaf. It has a piece of parchment paper on one end to protect it from drafts that would cause the leaf to blow away. It is used for holding and cutting the gold leaf or other metal leaf during the gilding process.

Gilder's tip. A flat brush made of a straight row of bristles held between two pieces of cardboard about 1 to 3 inches (3 to 8 cm) wide. It is used to pick up gold leaf and to place it on the surface to be gilded.

Gilding knife. A tool with a long narrow blade and a wood handle, but no cutting edge. It is used for handling and cutting the gold or other metal leaf in gilding projects.

Gimlet. A tool that consists of a steel shank with a screw thread at one end and a handle at the other for turning the tool. It is used for making holes in wood.

Glaze. A fine, transparent layer of paint that is applied to a surface to modify the tone or the shade.

Glue. Vegetable or animal substance that has water as a solvent and medium. Its main characteristic is the bonding power, which makes it useful as an adhesive or binder as well as for priming.

Glue (to). To bond two parts together using an adhesive.

Gouge. A chisel with a curved blade.

Grain. Thread or vein of the wood or marble that runs in one direction.

Graining comb. Plastic device with a toothed surface. It is used to make grain-like designs by dragging it across paint that is still wet.

Gum arabic. A product made from the excretions of different species of African acacia, especially the Arabia, from which it gets its name. It comes in granule form; when mixed with water it forms a sticky liquid that is used as a binder and additive in paint and as an adhesive in high concentrations.

h

Hand drill. A tool with a handle at one end and a drill bit at the other that is manually activated with a crank. It is used for boring holes.

Hydrogen peroxide. (H_2O_2). Substance that is used in concentrated form to bleach wood.

i

Inclusion. A substance that is completely surrounded and contained inside another.

Inert. An inert material is one that does not react when it comes in contact with other materials.

Inlay (to). To insert a piece or fragment of material (for example, wood, metal, bone, or ivory) into another material (wood) in such a way that it is permanently fixed in place.

Inlay wood. A sheet of thin wood whose thickness ranges between $5/32$ and $3/8$ inch (4 and 10 mm). It is used for inlay, which is done by inserting pieces into solid wood.

j

Jack plane. A tool similar to a plane, but larger and with a handle, which allows the application of greater force.

Joint. Union of two wood pieces where the protruding parts in one fit into the indentations of the other.

k

Knot. Hard growth that is formed where a branch meets the trunk of the tree.

l

Lacquer. Substance that is obtained from the excretions of *Rhus vernicifera*, a tree found in Japan, Borneo, Ceylon, and China. This material is hard to work with and requires great skill and effort. It is applied as surface coating following a technique of Japanese origin. It has a characteristic glossy finish and fine texture.

Latex. Product made from a mixture of synthetic, water-based resins. It is completely transparent and glossy when it dries. It is used as protection for wood or as an ingredient for paint.

Leaf. A fine sheet of beaten gold. Sold in booklets of $3 1/2$ inch (8 cm) and $5 1/2$ inch (14 cm) squares. The sheets are separated by protective pages in booklet form.

Linseed oil. Liquid obtained from crushing and pressing flax seeds. It is used to dilute paints and to provide a medium for pigments. It dries slowly and from the outside in.

Liquefy (to). The passage of a solid substance to a liquid state.

Marking gauge. A small block that has two adjustable arms attached to it, fitted with metal points at each end. It is used for making parallel lines on pieces of wood.

Medium. Vehicle that carries the binder and the pigment.

Metal leaf paint. A fine metallic powder that looks like gold and that is suspended in a transparent medium.

Mixer. Wide brush with short hair that is used in specific decorative techniques to blend edges.

Mixtion. Oily varnish made of linseed oil and additives. It does not dry completely and leaves a mordant. It is used for gilding, when the gold is left matte, unpolished.

Molding. Element with uniform relief and profile that is used as decoration. Available in both simple and compound forms.

Mop (ox-hair). Round brush (usually made of camel hair) that is used to arrange, brush off, or remove small pieces of gold leaf.

Mordant. Characteristic of certain adhesives, varnishes, and paints before they dry out completely; a sticky feel and, in certain cases, producing a peculiar sound when rubbed with the finger.

Mortise chisel. A chisel with a thick blade that ends in a bevel edge, between $3/32$ inch and $3/4$ inch (2 and 20 mm) wide. Its thickness matches its width. The total length ranges between 8 and 12 inches (20 and 30 cm). It is used by striking it with a mallet.

Oil paint. Term that designates the oil-based paints that have linseed oil as a medium and pigments.

Opaque. Coat of paint that does not let anything underneath through and, by extension, the color is not glossy or bright.

Overgrainer. Wide brush with divided ferrules forming different points. It is used in dragging and graining techniques.

Oxalic acid. (COOH) A chemical compound that is used in supersaturated solution to bleach wood or to even out its coloring.

Paint. Mixture of a binder and a pigment with mediums and additives, which results in a fluid substance that is easy to apply.

Paint layer. Each coat of paint that forms part of the decoration or that covers a surface.

Paint thinner. A solvent similar to essence of turpentine that is used in oil techniques.

Pastel. Solid mixture of pigments with a weak gum binder. It comes in small bars similar to pencils.

Patina. Tone, color, and quality that the surfaces of old objects acquire with the passage of time.

Pigment. Colored material to which no binder or medium has been added.

Plane. A tool made of a hard block of wood that has a steel cutting blade protruding from a crosswise slot. It is used for scraping, leveling, or smoothing wood.

Polychrome. Covering or decoration, usually painted, of an object that has many colors combined in an artistic configuration.

Precipitate (to). The separation of a substance in solid form from a supersaturated solution caused by adding more of it.

Press. Machine or tool used to press, bond, or compress an object between two parts.

Primer. The first layer applied to a surface that is to be decorated; it seals the pores and ensures the adhesion of subsequent layers.

Primer sealer. Paint that does not allow layers of paint or previous priming to show through and that, when applied to the base, does not produce significant irregularities.

Punch. This term is used to describe the small steel bars that have geometric motifs on

one end and that are used to decorate wood by tapping them with a mallet.

r

Resin. A natural substance that comes from different trees, or an artificial one made from chemical compounds. It is used as an adhesive or as an ingredient in varnish.

Respirator. Protective mask that covers the mouth and the nose and filters dust and harmful gases.

Root. The lower part of a plant that grows downward from the trunk, generally below the surface. It anchors the plant to the ground and absorbs water and nutrients.

Rough-hew (to). To remove the coarsest areas of an object. This term is also applied to the task of cutting wood with an adze to make boards.

Router plane. Tool used for reducing the surface of the wood evenly. It has a body fitted with two handles and a central hollow area where the interchangeable blades are attached with screws.

Rubbing pad. Small wad of fabric wrapped in a cloth. Used to apply a fine coat of varnish. Rubbing spreads the varnish and polishes at the same time.

S

Sander. Electric tool that has a rotating sandpaper disk or strip. It makes the sanding of large surfaces fast and easy.

Sanding. Rubbing a surface with sandpaper to make it smooth.

Sanding block. Block, usually made of cork, wrapped with sandpaper that acts as a base and makes it easier to hold.

Saturation. When a material is completely impregnated by another or when it can absorb no more of it.

Scalpel. Surgical tool that is used to make precise cuts. It is used in restoration mainly to remove material by scraping. There are different models with interchangeable blades to accommodate particular needs.

Scarf joint. Assembly of two pieces of wood attached at their ends.

Scraper. Tool made of a triangular steel sheet attached to a handle (usually made of wood) at its narrowest part. It is used for various tasks, such as scraping and applying putty.

Scraper blade. Steel sheet, generally rectangular or rounded in shape with sharp edges. It is used to smooth out flat surfaces by scraping while applying pressure with the hand.

Sealant. Commercial paint that is used to seal porous surfaces and that dries quickly.

Shellac. Weak resin that comes from India. It is available in flakes of different yellow and brown tones or in small white bars. It is soluble in alcohol and in water, and it is slightly alkaline.

Size. Commercial, water-based varnish that is used as an adhesive for the modern water gilding technique.

Sodium hypochlorite. Compound that has great bleaching power, used on various materials like wood and fabrics. It is also known as common bleach.

Solvent. Liquid that is added to paint, varnish, or wax. It can be water based or organic (such as essence of turpentine, alcohol, and mineral spirits).

Stable. A term used to describe a chemical compound that does not decompose easily.

Stain. Type of paint with liquid consistency and fine pigments that colors without covering, which leaves the quality and the grain of the wood visible.

Steel wool. Scrubbing pad made of metal fibers that is used to remove and to polish varnish.

Strip. Small, rectangular piece of wood, which is normally used for inlay. It is also called a band.

Supersaturated solution. Solution of one component dissolved in another that cannot absorb any more of the components, causing it to precipitate.

t

Tannic acid. Substance that is found in different parts of plants and that reacts in the presence of dyes. It is also known as gallic acid.

Tempera. Composition resulting from mixing water with one or several binders, to which pigments can be added to form paint.

Tessera. Small cubic shape made of any material that conforms to a mosaic-type composition.

Trunk. The part of the tree between the roots and the top.

V

Varnish. A solution of natural or synthetic gum or resin in a solvent that, when dry, forms a glossy, transparent, and waterproof surface.

Veining brush. Round brush with long hair that is used to paint veins.

Veneer. A thin sheet of wood, with a thickness ranging from $1/64$ to $3/16$ inch (0.2 to 5 mm), that is applied as a covering or decoration, using the techniques of marquetry and veneering.

Veneer hammer. Tool used to attach veneer. Its shape is similar to a conventional hammer, but its head is designed for applying pressure.

Veneer saw. Tool for sawing veneer. It consists of a steel blade that is $3/64$ or $3/32$ inch (1 or 2 mm) thick and 3 to 4 inches (7 to 10 cm) long, with teeth on both sides. It has a wooden handle on one end.

Veneering or marquetry tape. Narrow strip of fine perforated paper that has a weak adhesive, making it easy to remove.

Vise. Clamp.

Volatile. A term used to describe a substance that due to its inherent composition cannot stay in liquid form and evaporates easily.

W

Watercolor. Water-based paint made up of finely crushed pigments to which a binder (such as gum arabic, dextrine, fish glue, and tragacanth) is added, and substances that provide plasticity (such as glycerin and honey). Its main characteristic is its transparency.

Wax. Mineral, animal, or vegetable substances that have similar characteristics. They are used to give the wood the final finishing coat.

Whiting. White, inert pigment that is made of fine particles and is not opaque. It is used mainly for priming surfaces. It is also known as chalk, or Paris, Florence, or Meudon whiting.

Wood-burning iron. Electric tool with controlled heat used to decorate wood by darkening it. Has a transformer connected directly to the power source and a handle with interchangeable tips.

Wood filler. A toxic nitrocellulose varnish that is used for finishing wood and that seals the pores, resulting in a smooth surface.

Bibliography
and Acknowledgments

Allen, S. *Classic Finishing Techniques.* Sterling. New York, NY. 1995.

Brumbaugh, J. *Wood Furniture: Finishing, Refinishing, Repairing.* Macmillan. New York, NY. 1992.

Cavelle, S. *The Encyclopedia of Decorative Paint Techniques.* Running Press. Philadelphia, PA. 1994.

Chapman, A. *Learning the Art of Pyrography.* Schiffer Pub. Ltd. Atglen, PA. 1995.

Drucker, M. and Finkelstein, P. *Recipes for Surfaces.* Fireside. New York, NY. 1993.

Fine Woodworking Magazine Editors. *Veneering, Marquetry & Inlay.* Taunton. Newton, CT. 1996.

Finkelstein, P. *The Art of Faux.* Watson-Guptill Pub. New York, NY. 1997.

Frank, G. *Wood Finishing with George Frank.* Sterling. New York, NY. 1988.

Gibert, Vicenç. *Cabinetmaking.* Barron's Educational Series, Inc. Hauppauge, NY. 2000.

Gibert, Vicenç. *Marquetry.* Barron's Educational Series, Inc. Hauppauge, NY. 2000.

Gibert, Vicenç. *Restoration.* Barron's Educational Series, Inc. Hauppauge, NY. 2000.

Gloag, J. *A Complete Dictionary of Furniture.* Overlook Press. New York, NY. 1991.

Hayward, H. *World Furniture: An Illustrated History.* Random House Value. New York, NY. 1988.

Hoadley, R. *Identifying Wood: A Practical Handbook for Craftsmen.* Taunton Press. Newton, CT. 1990.

Hoadley, R. *Understanding Wood, A Craftsman's Guide to Wood Technology.* Taunton Press. Newton, CT. 2000.

Joyce, E. *Encyclopedia of Furniture Making.* Sterling. New York, NY. 1989.

Katz, S. *Hispanic Furniture: An American Collection.* Archit CT. Stamford, CT. 1986.

La Ferla, J. *Gilding.* Sterling. New York, NY. 1997.

Lincoln, Wm. *A Complete Manual of Wood Veneering.* Linden Pub. Fresno, CA. 1995.

Lincoln, Wm. *A World of Woods in Color.* Linden Pub. Fresno, CA. 1991.

Lucie-Smith, E. *Furniture: A Concise History.* Thames Hudson. New York, NY. 1985.

Pascual i Miró, E. *Restoring Wood.* Barron's Educational Series, Inc. Hauppauge, NY. 2000.

Sloan, A. *The Painted Furniture Sourcebook.* Rizzoli. New York, NY. 1998.

Smith, J. and DeBiere, J. *Restoration Recipes: A Paint Recipes Book.* Chronicle Books. San Francisco, CA. 1999.

Square, D. *The Veneering Book.* Taunton. Newton, CT. 1995.

To María Fernanda Canal for trusting us again with this project. To Joan Soto, Lucy, and her team of collaborators for their valuable advice in the preparation of the objects and processes that had to be photographed.

Mireia Campañà, Anna Jover, Josep Maria Miret, Eva Pascual, and Ana Ruiz de Conejo.

To Magda Gassó, Marc Salvador, and Josep Pascual for their invaluable trust, time, and support. To Isabel Juncosa for her patient help, to which I have resorted many times.

Eva Pascual